D0554652

UNIVERSITY OF NORTH CAROLINA

STUDIES IN COMPARATIVE LITERATURE

NUMBER 58

Luigi Pirandello

ON HUMOR

Introduced, Translated, and Annotated
by
ANTONIO ILLIANO
and
DANIEL P. TESTA

THE UNIVERSITY OF NORTH CAROLINA PRESS
CHAPEL HILL, N.C.

Text of *L'umorismo*
© Arnoldo Mondadori Editore, 1960

Library of Congress Cataloging in Publication Data

Pirandello, Luigi, 1867-1936.
  On humor.

  (University of North Carolina. Studies in compara-
tive literature, no. 58)
  Translation of L'umorismo.
  1. Wit and humor—History and criticism.
I. Illiano, Antonio, ed. II. Testa, Daniel P., ed.
III. Title. IV. Series: North Carolina. University.
Studies in comparative literature, no. 58.
PN6147.P513 1974   809.7   74-4281
ISBN 0-8078-7058-7

TABLE OF CONTENTS

TRANSLATORS' PREFACE

This translation of Pirandello's *L'umorismo* (Lanciano: Carabba, 1908; rev. ed., Florence: Battistelli, 1920) is based on the text of the essay as it appears in Pirandello's collected *Saggi, poesie, scritti varii,* ed. Manlio Lo Vecchio Musti (Milan: Mondadori, 1960). We have made slight revisions and corrections both in the text and in a few major prose quotations such as in the Leopardi passage in Chapter II, the citation from Barzellotti in Chapter IV, and the quotation from Rousseau in Part II. As for the quotations of poetry, we have revised the texts where it seemed appropriate and have supplied them with literal translations. Finally, we have revised and enlarged most of Pirandello's footnotes, and have provided new footnotes for numerous quotations which were left unidentified in the original text. The abbreviation [tr.] indicates the footnotes and other references supplied by the translators. With respect to Pirandello's indebtedness to Binet, Marchesini and Seailles in sections of Part Two, the reader should consult the studies by Franz Rauhut and Gösta Andersson.

A. I.
D. P. T.

INTRODUCTION

Luigi Pirandello's most significant contributions to modern literature came some fifty years ago with the staging of his *Six Characters in Search of an Author* (1921) and *Henry IV* (1922) in
successive European and American productions, which firmly
established the Sicilian writer as an original dramatist whose daring imagination challenged the theater audiences of the day. In
Six Characters, Pirandello dramatized the very forces underlying
drama and art and thereby shattered the conventions of the
realistic and naturalistic stage that were based on a well-made and
carefully-controlled dramatic plot. With *Henry IV,* a subtle work
that deals, on one of its levels, with role-playing and the theme of
madness, Pirandello seemed to give the stage the serious and expansive dimensions it had not had since the great dramatic conceptions
of seventeenth century baroque theater. Those two plays were as
responsible as any for banishing from the European stage its linger-
ing emphasis on the bourgeois way of life and the superficial
banter that was often used to represent the drama of that society.
Liberated from the fossilized elements of tradition, the theater
joined the other media of art in pursuing forms that were more
radically experimental and innovative.

But if Pirandello's international acclaim was due principally to
two plays that he wrote when he was already over fifty years old,
his genuinely original work as an artist and thinker predates that
triumph by at least twenty years, when he was writing short and
long fiction as well as poetry, and when he began seriously to set
down his critical and esthetic ideas in essay form. One needs only
to mention that perhaps his best novel, *Il fu Mattia Pascal,* was
published in 1904, and represents, in view of that early date, an
astonishing achievement. With *Il fu Mattia Pascal,* Pirandello
moves away from his early naturalistic interests and away from the
nineteenth century's preoccupation with the historical and societal
forces that exert an oppressive influence on man or diminish his

dignity and autonomy. In this novel and in many subsequent works, Pirandello creates situations which exist inside his characters rather than situations in which the characters are placed, a kind of inner realism that attempts to dramatize the dynamism of the self. The themes we claim to see in Pirandello's works are not, strictly speaking, themes at all, that is, they are not intellectual presentations, but rather dramatic embodiments of human interiority. This obsession with depth psychology and with the levels of human personality is what gives Pirandello's work its striking modern note, and reveals his innate interest in an area of study that had just begun to receive serious scientific attention. Unlike some of the naturalists, Pirandello makes no pretense of being a scientist, although he cites with approval a work such as Alfred Binet's *Les altérations de la personnalité,* which presents a wide range of fascinating psychological experiments and observations on human subjects. In addition, at least one aspect of Pirandello's personal life—his wife's mental sickness—contributed to his intense and enduring concern for the study of certain critical aspects and problems of the human character.

Pirandello's essays express a similar impulse to re-evaluate certain traditional notions about literature and to develop and defend his new ideas not only as a detached thinker or critic but also as a creative writer with a passionate commitment to his art. His major essay, *L'umorismo* (1908), which is being presented in this volume for the first time in its entirety in English translation, has long been recognized as the most complete statement of Pirandello's esthetic, and as such, it has been often mentioned in connection with his creative work. What is important, however, is that the essay is not simply a synthesis of Pirandello's basic ideas about art and life (for Pirandello, the two are inextricably bound), but rather an illuminating record of an arduous literary and critical experience that helped him reach a brilliant elucidation of his thought and of his mission as a writer. The wide range of subjects that Pirandello utilizes is significantly revealing both with respect to the essay's form and style and with respect to his conception of literature and reality.

In his essay on humor Pirandello treats a subject which engaged his thinking even as a young writer of poetry. It was in Germany, however, that he discovered a vast critical tradition devoted to comedy, humor, and irony—a tradition which stemmed mainly from the great writers of the romantic period. Although the doctrine of romantic irony confirmed for Pirandello the underlying structure of antithesis in life, there were certain aspects of that doctrine which did not satisfy his temperament: ᵉe.g., the notion that the ironic writer is detached from, and even superior to, the world he creates, was alien to his own deepest feelings as an artist. After his return to Italy, his reading, teaching, and writing were largely directed toward developing his own view of humor. During this time, he eventually came to understand that humor was the literary mode to which his own creative temperament was most intimately attuned.

Pirandello's treatise on humor not only incorporates ideas developed many years earlier, but it points toward his later works and provides the germinating idea for many of them. Not an essay in the strict sense, the work is rather a lively mosaic of argumentation and polemics, critical insights, penetrating analysis, and finally a profound poetic exposition of life, all of which clearly establish an organic relationship between the essay itself and the rest of Pirandello's works. It is also no wonder that the author's presentation of ideas, enmeshed as they are with his creative temperament, should have been judged confusing by the rationalistic philosopher of esthetics, Benedetto Croce.

The work, however, is far from confusing if we are prepared to follow the author's historical excursus which attempts to establish a strictly defined tradition of humor that will satisfy both a creative temperament and rational criteria. Pirandello himself sensed that before he would be in a position to formulate his own concept of humor—a concept that evolves from romanticism, but, as we shall see, is distinctively and originally modern—he would need to engage himself in a critical analysis which would trace the sources of a misunderstanding both with respect to the true definition of humor and to the problem of identifying the true humorists among the great writers of the past. This effort amounted to a clarification that was helpful not only for his readers but for his own development as critic and writer. The first six chapters take up various topics and issues which, although sometimes only peripherally related, are stimulating to read and reveal a penetrating and committed critical mind at work. In his typically polemical manner, Pirandello blames the strong Italian rhetorical tradition for inhibiting the inner freedom that the creative spirit needs in order to express itself in its full originality; he severely criticizes the neo-classical school, the practice of imitation, and the prestige of formal art for obstructing the growth of regional or folk poetry and, at times, the unique expressions of authentic humor. On the other hand, Pirandello is able to recognize and defend Italy's contribution to Western humor. Never blatantly parochial, Pirandello's literary and historical judgment serves as a reasonable corrective to the then-prevalent view that Italian letters were devoid of true humor and that the authentic humorists, with a few exceptions, were to be found only in the Nordic countries. Pirandello's defense of Italian humor must not be taken, therefore, as an expression of a narrowly nationalistic attitude; it must be placed within the context of his balanced and convincing argument that humor understood in its proper sense cuts across national frontiers and is not exclusive of any period. We can thus accept the outline of Italian humor (Chapter VI) as an account that is both reliable and effective in its lively and personal approach. If, on the one hand, he praises the little known Calabrian writer, Giovanni Merlino, one of whose volumes was written "for those with limited intelligence who want effective instruction on how to lose it completely," he argues, on the other hand, with accuracy and coherence, that some of the great Italian writers like Machiavelli, Giordano Bruno, and Manzoni should be classed with the most authentic humorists.

The longest chapter of the first part of Pirandello's essay is largely a survey of Italian chivalric poetry of the Renaissance that, while cast in negative terms, is of the utmost importance since it shows how the author put to the test his critical thoughts on the subject of humor and its intimate relationship to other concepts like burlesque, satire, and irony. He finds Ariosto's and Boiardo's artistic purpose more "serious" than Pulci's, but the dominant mode of their major works is comic irony. In this analysis Pirandello's critical use of irony is partly based on Schlegel's definition that irony reduces the artistic matter to a perpetual parody in which the author never loses, even in those moments of pathos, his awareness of the unreality of his own creation. Even in the case of Ariosto, however, who for Pirandello is the most accomplished stylist of the three poets, there is lacking the essential ingredient that would have made him an authentic humorist. What Ariosto finally fails to do is to "dramatize" his comic sense of reality, since he does not fuse the comic elements with the tragic elements, both of which are present in the work but remain consistently separated. The work in which this fusion is successfully achieved is *Don Quijote,* which, together with Manzoni's *I promessi sposi,* is judged by Pirandello to be one of the most exemplary works of humor.

Pirandello's limitation of romantic irony *vis-a-vis* humor seems to imply that, as long as the ironist holds to a position of superiority and distance between himself as creator and the world of his characters, he denies himself the experience of penetrating to the deepest levels of his being; in short, he fails to transcend his role as artist. The humorist, instead, drawing from a more inward source of experience, discovers that he too, like his projections, is "human," that is, easily deceived and blinded by suprahuman forces and passions; he cannot help, if he is honest, but infuse a more emotional content, a greater psychic energy, into his literary creation. In an interesting speculative interpretation of Cervantes, Pirandello posits, with the help of that writer's biography, an existential crisis in which the Spanish writer was able suddenly and dramatically to see his life in terms of a radical conflict between his former ideal self as expressed in patriotic and religious actions and his present naked self that perceives a real world devoid of those illusions. That crisis is what accounts for the bitter disillusionment that underlies the *Quijote* and what instilled in the author the "feeling of the opposite," which, as Pirandello explains in the second part of the essay, is the distinctive trait of the true humorist. That the example of the *Quijote* with its irreducible ambivalent nature continued to intrigue Pirandello is borne out by the comments made in the section of Part Two where the Italian author explains how the "feeling of the opposite" makes its effect on the sensitive reader of the *Quijote:* our first inclination is to laugh at the mad capers of the principal character, but because his aspirations are towards justice and his actions have a personal heroic quality, there simultaneously arises in us "a feeling of pity, of sorrow, and of admiration," which troubles or hampers our laughter and "makes it bitter."

The traditional identification of humor with laughter is transcended by the Pirandellian view of humor, for Pirandello holds that humorists do not try to make people laugh—a notion he had already expressed in an essay published on Cecco Angiolieri in 1896. Laughter, for Pirandello, falls naturally in the province of the comic, which he calls the "perception of the opposite," and which, if it is to achieve its effect, will not seek deeper feelings nor penetrate to underlying motivations. Humor, on the other hand, with its "feeling of the opposite," touches a deeper base where it is able to perceive simultaneously the conflicting aspects of every situation: faced with a comic situation it will perceive its serious side, and vice versa. This "feeling of the opposite" is made possible by a "special activity of reflection," which Pirandello considers a crucial element in the creative process of humor. Pirandello's concept of humoristic reflection has little to do with reflection as conscious thought and meditation, or with reflection as it functions in the work of any non-humorous writer. For Pirandello, humoristic reflection is an impulsive and spontaneous force which works from within the creative process, disturbing and disrupting the movement of images by evoking "an association through contraries," so that "the images, instead of being linked through similarity or juxtaposition, are presented in conflict." Because of this special kind of reflection which is inherent in the humoristic temperament, the humorist is a man with a double nature, a man whose condition is to be constantly off key "like a violin and double bass at the same time." What the artistic imagination creates, reflection in its critical role undoes, "resembling a diabolical imp that takes apart the mechanism of each image, of each phantasm produced by the emotions; it takes it apart in order to see how it is made; it releases the mainspring, and the whole mechanism squeaks convulsively." This double nature reveals itself also in the very style of Pirandello's essay, a style which constantly alternates between theoretical statement and intuitive criticism. For example, in differentiating between reflection in any non-humorous writer and reflection in the humorist, Pirandello says that in the former, reflection "is almost a form of feeling, almost a mirror in which feeling looks at itself," but when the artistic temperament is naturally humoristic, that mirror of reflection consists of "icy water, in which the flame of feeling not only looks at itself but also plunges in it and extinguishes itself."

What, finally, does Pirandello say about the deeper meaning underlying the unique mode of being that is the humorist's? He makes it clear that he rejects any notion that would assign to the work of art a determining cause (see his discussion of Lipps' ethical considerations) since, for him, artistic creativity arises spontaneously and ingenuously. Nonetheless, in some of the most inspired pages of his essay, he moves, in an ever-expanding and rapidly shifting frame of reference, to wider and deeper perspectives that not only bore inwardly to those areas of being hidden from the rational self but also point outwardly to the realm of the transcendental. Pirandello argues that man continually fabricates illusions about himself and about reality because he needs to give a meaning and a coherence to his life and to the world. Thus it is that man cloaks his empty reality with his mental constructions and with the abstracting work of logic. Because the humorist is endowed with a special activity of reflection, his role is to tear the masks away and remind man of the harsh reality of his predicament. He does it with compassion and pain even when he laughs, and with a keen awareness that life resists fixed forms and ideal concepts and is forever unyielding to any rational explanation. That shadow of pessimism which is cast by so many of Pirandello's fictional and dramatic works finds its explicit expression in Part Two of the essay where he says that "man . . . is given at birth the sad privilege of feeling himself alive, with the fine illusion that results from it: that of taking this inner feeling, changeable and varying, as something that really exists outside of himself."

This succinct and existentially difficult truth, as it finally unfolds from Pirandello's critical gropings, is seen to be the source of man's fundamental sense of anguish and is the basis of his self-delusions. But even after he has grasped the painful truth about his limitations, it is with that very spark of life that man will forever strive to transcend himself in questioning the enormous mystery that surrounds him and in perceiving, fleetingly at times and always without final assurances, the hazy outlines of a higher order of truth, as Pirandello himself so brilliantly demonstrates with his philosophical and poetic insights into man's relation to the cosmos, in a passage which could be defined as one of the most original re-interpretations of the myth of Prometheus in the twentieth century.

It should be fairly evident even from the foregoing remarks, as certainly a direct reading of the essay will reveal, that Pirandello's probings into a complex subject cannot be properly evaluated as a systematic exposition and a thoroughly objective theory of humor. Yet, Pirandello, like other writers who were also critics, remains faithful to his creative temperament and to his view of the human soul as a problematical, ever-changing entity that cannot be reduced to oneness. Shunning the path of abstract concepts, Pirandello lets his intelligence work in close harmony with his intuition and empirical perception, and thus is able constantly to penetrate within the inner structure of the human self and to achieve a unique understanding of the life of the human soul, which forms the basis of his conception of humor.

A. I.
D. P. T.

PART ONE

Chapter I. THE WORD *HUMOR*

In his well known study on Cecco Angiolieri, Alessandro D'Ancona explains how extensive the element of burlesque is in the work of the thirteenth century poet from Siena. "And yet," he adds, "it is my view that Angiolieri is not simply a burlesque writer; it would be more appropriate to consider him a *humorist* as well. This may indeed cause the guardians of language to frown, but they cannot claim that in Italian we must forego mentioning a particular thing only because we have no word for it."[1] In a footnote he then aptly points out: "How odd it is that a French translator of a German dissertation on humor should maintain that, although the British, and particularly Congreve, have claimed for themselves the words humor and humorist, it is nonetheless true that they come from Italian."[2] And D'Ancona goes on to say: "Furthermore, in Italian *umore* means also *fantasia, capriccio,* and *umorista* means also *fantastico;* and everybody knows that the 'humors' of the mind and the soul are closely related to Italian 'humoristic' poetry. In times past Italy had the academies of the *Umorosi* in Bologna and Cortona and the academy of the *Umoristi* in Rome, and let us hope that the bad humors of politics will never cause Italy to lose the 'fine and graceful humors' of art."[3]

[1] Alessandro D'Ancona, *Studi di critica e storia letteraria* (Bologna: Zanichelli, 1880), pp. 178–79.

[2] Cf. "Humour" in *Recueil de pièces intéressantes, concernant les antiquités, les beaux-arts, les belles-lettres et la philosophie, traduites de différentes langues* (Paris, Strasbourg, the Hague, 1787), Vol. 1, 375–87; the unnamed French translator makes that statement while citing Riedel's article "Laune," Vol. I of his *Theorie der schönen Künste und Wissenschaften.*

[3] Naples also had academies: cf. *Archivio storico per le provincie napoletane,* V, 608. And why not mention also the "Accademia degli Umidi" of Florence, "whose happy-go-lucky members were bound by traditional practice to a burlesque style which was happy, joyous, amiable, and inspired good comradeship," as Lasca says in his letter to Lorenzo Scala which prefaces the first book of his burlesque works (Bern: Giunta, 1548)? For the terms *umore* and *umorismo,* see also Baldensperger's "Les définitions de l'humour," in his *Etudes d'histoire littéraire* (Paris: Hachette, 1907), pp. 176–222, Spingarn's introduction to the first volume of his *Critical Essays of the Seventeenth Century* (Oxford: Clarendon Press, 1908), and Croce's remarks in *Critica,* VII (1909), 219–20.

1

The word *umore* derives naturally from Latin *humor,* which designated a physical substance in the form of fluid, liquid, humidity or moisture. It was also used in the sense of fantasy, whim, and vigor: for instance, when Plautus says, "I have a good deal of humor in my body and I am not as yet exhausted from beautiful and pleasurable things,"[4] he obviously does not imply any physical connotation for we know that since ancient times bodily humors were considered to be symptoms and causes of illness. One can read in an old book of veterinary medicine that "humans have four humors—blood, bile, phlegm, and melancholy—and these humors are the cause of man's sicknesses."[5] And in Brunetto Latini: "Melancholy is a humor which many call black bile and it is cold, dry, and has its seat in the spine," an opinion that had already been expressed by Cicero and Pliny.[6] St. Augustine informs us in one of his sermons that "leek inflames the bile and cabbage produces melancholy."[7]

It will be well, in treating the subject of humor, to keep in mind that the word humor also meant sickness; and that, before acquiring the sense of delicate emotion or inner feeling that it has for us today, melancholy originally meant bile or gall and the ancients understood it in the physical sense of the word. We shall see later the relation that the two words humor and melancholy have after they acquired a psychological meaning. Meanwhile, let us say that this relationship, while definitely never lacking in the spirit of the Italian language, failed to manifest itself clearly. In fact, for us, the word humor has preserved the physical meaning, as evidenced by a Tuscan proverb that draws its example from watery fruit: "Chi ha umore non ha sapore" ("He who has humor has no flavor"); on the other hand, whenever it takes on a psychological meaning, it does express inclination, nature, disposition, temporary state of mind, and even fantasy, thought, or whim, but

---

[4] Plautus, *Miles gloriosus,* III, 1, 44–45. [tr.]

[5] On the four humors of the body cf also Vindicianus Afer, *Epistula ad Pentadium, nepotem suum,* and Isidorus, *Etymologiarum Lib. IV:* De Medecina, 5. [tr.]

[6] Cicero, *Tusc.* 5. 11.; Brunetto Latini, *Li livres dou tresor,* I, Pt. III, 102. Cf. "melancholia" in H. Stephano, *Thesaurus Linguae Graecae,* V. [tr.]

[7] Cf. C. Plinius Secundus, *Naturalis Historia,* XX, 36. [tr.] Cecco Angiolieri, in one of his sonnets, after listing some of the harmful foods suggested to him by his mother who hates him, says: "E se di questo non avessi voglia/e stessi quasimente su la colla/molto mi loda porri con la foglia" ("And if I don't feel like eating it and show myself unwilling to accept, then she sings the praises of fresh leek to me").

it lacks any specific connotation and must therefore be used together with adjectives such as *tristo, gaio, tetro, buono, cattivo,
bello* (sad, cheerful, somber, good, bad, witty). In short the Italian
word *umore* does not correspond to the English *humour*. The
English word, as Tommaseo says, is a combination and blend of
the expressions *bell'umore, buonumore,* and *malumore;* in other
words, it has something to do with St. Augustine's cabbages.

We are here talking about the word and not the thing itself. It
is important to point this out, because we wouldn't want anyone
to think that the Italians lack the thing itself merely because the
Italian word failed to incorporate and keep on the conceptual
level what was already part of its original physical meaning. We
shall see that it all comes down to a need for Italians to make
clearer distinctions because, whether witty, good, somber, or cheerful, Italian humor is always humor and it does not differ in essence
from its English counterpart but in the modifications that naturally
are stamped on it by a different language and by the varied
temperaments of its writers.

Moreover, let no one think that the English word *humour* and
its Italian derivative *umorismo* are so easy to understand. In his
essay on Angiolieri, to which we shall return shortly, D'Ancona
himself confesses: "If I were to give a definition of *umorismo,* I
would really have a great deal of difficulty." And he is right. That's
what everybody says: "Piuttosto no 'l comprendo, che te 'l dica"
("I rather say I don't understand it than tell you"). Baldensperger
speaks about all the definitions of humor attempted in the eighteenth and nineteenth centuries and, like Croce, comes to the conclusion that "there is no such thing as humor, there are only
humorists,"[8] as if one could identify a humorist without first having some idea of what humor is, as if it sufficed merely to uphold
the view (as does Cazamian, quoted by Baldensperger himself) that
humor escapes the grasp of science because its constant and typical
traits are scarce and, above all, negative, whereas its variable elements are countless. Even Addison considered it easier to say what
humor is not, rather than what it is. And all the laborious efforts
that have been expended, up to the present, to define humor, truly
call to mind those most specious seventeenth century attempts at
defining *ingegno* (just think of Emmanuele Tesauro's *Cannocchiale
aristotelico*), *gusto* or *buon gusto,* and that ineffable "something"

---

[8] Baldensperger, p. 217.

about which Bouhours wrote: "The Italians, who make a mystery of everything, always resort to their *non so che:* nothing appears more frequently in their poets."[9] The Italians "make a mystery of everything"! But just ask the French what they mean by *esprit.*

As for humor, D'Ancona goes on to say:

It is true that to give a definition is not easy because humor has innumerable manifestations which vary according to country, period, and poetic temperament, and that the humor of Rabelais and Merlin Cocai is not identical to that of Sterne, Swift, or Jean Paul Richter; likewise Heine's humoristic vein differs from Musset's. Perhaps in no other literary endeavour does (or should) a more subtle distinction exist between verse and prose as in humor, although the readers and even the writers do not always perceive it. But this is not the place to discuss such a distinction, or what causes it, or the differing traits that characterize humor, satire, epigram, jest, parody, and the various forms of the comic. Nor is this the place to decide whether or not some humorists are merely "lunatics," as Richter puts it. One thing is certain, however: all those referred to as humorists by public opinion have fundamentally something in common.[10]

The observation is essentially accurate, but—be careful with public opinion!—we should like to tell D'Ancona. "After the word romanticism," Enrico Nencioni says,

humor is the most abused and misused word in Italy [*only in Italy?*]. If all the Italian writers, books, and newspapers classified as humorous were truly so, we would have nothing to envy the countries of Sterne and Thackeray, Richter and Heine. We could not step out of the house without running into a couple of Cervanteses and a dozen Dickenses . . . We merely wish to indicate from the very beginning that a Babylonian confusion exists in the interpretation of the word *umorismo*. For the majority, a humorist is a writer who makes people laugh: a writer of comedy, burlesque, satire, trivia, and grotesque. Caricature, farce, epigrams, and puns are all designated as humor; similarly the term *romantic* has long been applied to everything that is most Arcadian and sentimental, false and baroque. Paul de Kock is confused with Dickens, and the Viscount d'Arlincourt with Victor Hugo.

The above is what Enrico Nencioni pointed òut, already in 1884, in an article entitled precisely "L'umorismo e gli umoristi,"[11] which caused quite a stir. It cannot truly be said that public opinion during all this time has changed. Even today the humorist

9 Dominique Bouhours, "Le je ne scay quoi," *Les entretiens d'Ariste et d'Eugene,* ed. Ferdinand Brunot (Paris: Librairie Armand Colin, 1962), p. 144. The work was first published in Paris, 1671. [tr.]

10 D'Ancona, p. 179–80.

11 Enrico Nencioni, "L'umorismo e gli umoristi," *Nuova Antologia,* 73 (1884), 193–211, also in his *Saggi critici* (Florence, 1898), pp. 175–202.

is, for the general public, a writer who makes people laugh. But, I
repeat, why only in Italy? It is true everywhere! The masses cannot
understand the concealed contrasts, the exquisite subtleties of true
humor. Caricature, extravagant farce, and the grotesque are often
mistaken for authentic humor; they are even mistaken in countries
where it seemed to Nencioni (and not only to him) that humor is
at home. Isn't it true that Mark Twain is called a humorist, although his short stories are, in his own definition, "good things,
immensely funny sayings and stories that will bring a smile upon
the gruffest countenance"?[12]

Journalism, a certain kind of journalism, has seized, adopted,
and, going to any length to provide coarse laughter, popularized
the word in this false sense, so that every true humorist today will
consent to be identified as such only with some reluctance and
even indignation: 'A humorist, indeed, but . . . let's not confuse
it—' he feels the need to warn, 'a humorist *in the true sense of
the word.*' As if to say: 'My intention, you see, is not to make you
laugh by playing verbal pranks.' And more than one writer, in
order to avoid being taken for a buffoon and classed among the
thousands of fourth-rate humorists, have discarded the worn out
expression, and, leaving it to the people, have adopted, instead,
ironismo, ironista. Just as from *umore,* we have *umorismo,* so from
ironia, we get *ironismo.*

But irony, in what sense? Here again we will have to make a
distinction, for irony has both a rhetorical and a philosophical
connotation. As a rhetorical figure, irony involves a deception
which is absolutely contrary to the nature of genuine humor. It is
true that this rhetorical figure implies a contradiction, but only an
apparent one, between what is said and what is meant.

The contradiction of humor is never, on the other hand, an
apparent one, but rather an essential one, as we shall see, and one
quite different in nature. Dante, for instance, uses rhetorical irony
when he excludes from the crowd of the sinners those who are
most blameworthy, as in "ogn'uom v'è barattier, fuor che Bonturo"
(*Inf.* XXI.41, "everyone there is a swindler except Bonturo") and
as in the case of the mad prodigals (*Inf.* XXIX.121–132), where
to the poet's question, "Or fu giammai / gente così vana . . .
("Now was there ever a people so vain"), one of the condemned

---

[12] Samuel L. Clemens, *Eye openers, good things, immensely funny sayings
. . . by Mark Twain* [pseud.] . . . (London: Ward, Lock and Tyler, [1875]).
[tr.]

replies, "Tra'mene Stricca . . . e tra'ne la brigata" ("Except Stricca
. . . and except the company"). Dante again uses rhetorical irony
when he recalls what was good in life in order to exacerbate the
present suffering, as in the case of the devils who shout at a
swindler from Lucca:

. . . Qui non ha luogo il Santo Volto:
qui si nuota altrimenti che nel Serchio! (*Inf.* XXI.48–49)

(Here the Sacred Face has no place:
here the swimming is not like in the Serchio!);

or when he has a speaker stress his own merits by asserting them
in a rough and cutting fashion as in the case of the devil who takes
a soul away from St. Francis through theological argumentation
about penance, so that the captured soul ends up having to hear
the devil's remark, "Forse/tu non pensavi ch'io loico fossi!" (*Inf.*
XXVII.122–123, "Perhaps you didn't think I was so good at
logic!"); or when he exclaims: "Godi, Fiorenza, poi che se' sí
grande" (*Inf.*XXVI.1, "Be joyful, Florence, since you are so
great"), and:

Fiorenza mia, ben puoi esser contenta
di questa digression che non ti tocca,
. . .
Or ti fa' lieta, ché tu hai ben onde:
tu ricca, tu con pace, tu con senno! (*Purg.* VI.127–137)

(Oh, my Florence, you may indeed be happy
with this digression which touches you not,
. . .
Now be of good cheer, for you have good reason:
you who are rich, at peace, and so wise!).

When Dante writes like this, he gives admirable examples of irony
in the rhetorical sense, and yet neither in them nor in any other
passage of the *Commedia* can one find a trace of humor.

   Another meaning, we said, a philosophical one, was given to the
word *irony* in Germany. Friedrich Schlegel and Ludwig Tieck
derived it directly from Fichte's subjective idealism, though it ultimately stems from the whole post-Kantian idealistic and romantic
movement. The Self, the only true reality, Hegel explained, can
laugh at the vain appearance of the universe; since it can create
this appearance, it can also abolish it. The Self can choose not to
take its own creation seriously, hence irony—a force which, according to Tieck, enables the poet to dominate his subject matter

and because of which, says Friedrich Schlegel, the subject matter turns into a perpetual parody, a transcendental farce.

Transcendental indeed, I should say, is this conception of irony, and after all, considering its source, it could not have been otherwise. Still, romantic irony is, or, at least in a certain sense, can be related to, true humor and it certainly is more closely akin to true humor than rhetorical irony. Eventually romantic irony could even be made to derive from rhetorical irony, though not without some strain: in the latter one should not take seriously what is said while in the former one can choose not to take seriously what is done. As compared to romantic irony, rhetorical irony would be like the famous frog of the fable which—having been carried into the contrived world of German metaphysical idealism and filling itself up more with air than with water—would successfully attain the enviable dimensions of an ox. The deception—that apparent contradiction of which rhetoric speaks—has here become, by dint of the continual swelling, the vain appearance of the universe. Now if humor consisted exclusively of the pin prick which deflates the blown-up frog, then irony and humor would be approximately the same thing. But humor, as we shall see, is more than just that puncture.

As usual, Friedrich Schlegel did nothing more than to exaggerate someone else's ideas and theories: not only the subjective idealism of Fichte but also the famous theory of the play instinct expounded by Schiller in the twenty-seven letters of his *Ueber die aesthetische Erziehung des Menschen*. Fichte's intention was, after all, to complete the Kantian doctrine of duty. By stating that the universe is created by the spirit, by the Self—which is also divinity, the soul of the world's essence, the spirit that engenders everything and is impersonal, and the untiring will that encloses within itself reason, freedom and morality—Fichte had intended to show that the duty of the individual was to submit to the will of the whole and to strive for the highest degree of moral harmony.

Now, the Self conceived by Fichte became the individual 'self', the small, erratic self of Mr. Friedrich Schlegel, who with a bubble pipe and soapy water started merrily puffing up bubbles—vain appearances of the universe, worlds—and blowing them out of existence. This was his game. Poor Schiller! His *Spieltrieb* could not have been misrepresented in a more unworthy fashion. But Mr. Schlegel took literally Schiller's words: "Man should only *play* with beauty and should play *only* with beauty. Thus, to say it once and for all, man plays only when he is man in the full sense of the word, and he is man in the full sense of the word only when he plays,"[13] and said that irony consists in the poet's never identifying himself completely with his own work, in his remaining fully aware, even in the moments of pathos, of the unreality of his creations, in not becoming the stooge of the phantoms created by his own imagination, and in laughing at the reader who is drawn into the game and also at himself who devotes his life to playing.[14]

Once irony is understood in this sense, one can easily see how it is mistakenly attributed to certain writers like Manzoni, for example, who made a veritable obsession of objective reality and historical truth, to the point of finding fault with his own masterpiece. On the other hand, the other type of irony—the rhetorical—cannot be attributed to Manzoni either, since no contradiction that is a contradiction only in appearance is ever to be found in his work between what he says and what he means. Such a contradiction is the result of indignation, and Manzoni never becomes indignant with reality when it conflicts with his ideal. He compromises here and there out of compassion and is often indulgent, presenting in each case, vividly and in detail, the reasons for his compromises and indulgence: and this, as we shall see, is a characteristic of humor.

It would therefore seem unwarranted to replace *umorismo, umorista* with *ironismo, ironista*. Even when irony is employed towards a good end, one cannot remove from it the notion of a certain *mockery* and *mordancy*, two qualities that may also be found in writers who are unquestionably humorists but whose humor will certainly not consist of such biting mockery. Nevertheless, we have to take into account the fact that the meaning of words can be altered by common consent and that in current usage many words have a meaning which differs from the meaning they had in the past. Consequently, if—as we saw—the meaning of the word humor has really changed already, then there would essentially be nothing wrong in adopting a new word that can establish and define the meaning of its object unequivocably.

---

[13] F. Schiller, *Ueber die aesthetische Erziehung des Menschen,* letter 15.
[14] Cf. Victor Basch, *La poétique de F. Schiller* (Paris: Alcan, 1902), pp. 284–85.

Chapter II. PRELIMINARY QUESTIONS

Before we begin to talk about the essence, characteristics, and substance of humor, we need to clear the ground of three preliminary questions: 1) Is humor, as a literary phenomenon, exclusively modern? 2) Is it foreign to the Italians? 3) Is it peculiarly Nordic? On one hand, these questions are closely related to the broader and more complex question of the difference between modern art and ancient art—a question argued at length during the controversy over classicism and romanticism; on the other hand, they are connected with romanticism, which was considered by the Anglo-Germanic peoples as their victorious reprisal over the classicism of the Latins. In fact, we shall see that the various controversies on humor make use of the same arguments of romantic criticism, beginning with those used by Schiller who, according to Goethe, founded all of modern aesthetics with his famous *Uber naive und sentimentalisce Dichtung*.[1]

Those arguments are well known: the subjectivism in the speculative-sentimental poet, representative of modern art, as opposed to the objectivism in the instinctive or ingenuous poet, representative of ancient art; the contrast between the ideal and the real; the imperturbable composure, the poised dignity, the outer beauty of ancient art as opposed to the exaltation of the emotions, the vagueness, the infinity, the indeterminateness of aspirations, the melancholic longings, the nostalgia, the inner beauty of modern art; the veristic earthiness of ingenuous poetry versus the hazy abstractions and intellectual dizziness of sentimental poetry;[2] the impact of Christianity; the philosophical element; the incoherence of modern art as opposed to the harmony

[1] Johann Wolfgang von Goethe, *Zur Naturwissenschaft im Allgemeinen*, in *Werke* (Berlin: Hempel, 1868–79), vol. XXXIV, 96–97. But Goethe did not take into account the fact that Herder had distinguished between *Natur-poesie* and *Kunst-poesie* before Schiller. See also Victor Basch, *La poétique de F. Schiller* (Paris: Alcan, 1902).

[2] Cf. G. Muoni, *Note per una poetica storica del romanticismo* (Milan: Società editrice libraria, 1906), p. 8.

9

of Greek poetry; the individualized particularities set against classical typification; reason that concerns itself more with the philosophical value of content than with the beauty of external form; the deep-felt sense of an inner disunity and double nature typical of modern man, etc. This can be substantiated partly by a passage from Nencioni's "L'umorismo e gli umoristi," which we had occasion to mention earlier:

Antiquity, in its fine balance of senses and emotions, looked with dispassionate poise also into the tragic abyss of destiny. The human soul was then young and healthy and neither the heart nor intelligence had yet been tormented by thirty centuries of precepts, systems, sufferings and doubts: no sorrowful doctrines or inner crises had disturbed the serene harmony of human life and spirit. But time and Christianity had taught modern man to think about infinity and to compare it to the ephemeral and painful breath of present life. Our organism is constantly excited and overexcited, and secular afflictions have "humanized" our hearts. We look into the human soul and into nature with a more penetrating sympathy, and we find in them mysterious relations and an intimate poetry unknown to the ancients. . . . Aristophanes' comic imagination and artistic laughter and a few of Lucian's dialogues are exceptions. Antiquity did not and could not have a humoristic literature. . . . The latter, it seems, is characteristic of the literatures of the English and Germans. The dim sky and the moist soil of the North seem to be more suitable for nourishing the strange and delicate plant of humor.[3]

Nencioni conceded however that "also under the blue sky and in the easy life of the Latin peoples" humor "has at times flourished, and in a few instances uniquely and splendidly." He spoke in fact of Rabelais and Cervantes, of Carlo Porta's "realistic and living" humor and of Carlo Bini, whose humor he called "delicate and desolate," and considered Manzoni's Don Abbondio a first-rate humoristic creation.[4]

More uncompromising in his negative appraisal was Giorgio Arcoleo. While admitting that humor, though peculiar to modern literature, does not lack ties with antiquity, and while quoting Socrates' teaching that "the origin of happiness and sadness is one and the same: in an antithesis the first idea can only be known through its opposite, so that tragedy and comedy are made of the same stuff," he went on to add:

This the Greek intellect formulated as thought, but Art was unable to express it: the perception of opposites remained in the realm of the

<hr />

[3] Enrico Nencioni, "L'umorismo e gli umoristi," *Nuova Antologia*, 73 (1884), 193–211, also in his *Saggi critici* (Florence, 1898), pp. 175–202.
[4] *Ibid.* [tr.]

abstract because life was different. Theogony wrapped the soul in myth, the Epic wrapped human deeds in legend, and Politics wrapped the power of individuals in the supreme law of the State. Antiquity did unperturbably compress abstract forms in the harmony of the finite world: it perceived either the Cyclops or the Gnome, the Graces or the Parcae. As life had either free men or slaves, all-powerful or powerless men, so science had laughter or tears, Heraclitus or Democritus, and literature had tragedies or comedies. At best, the sense of contrast made its way from the sphere of the intellect to that of the imagination where it became a phantasy; this is when Aristophanes satirized the sophists and Lucian the Gods. But if Paganism had become deeply engrossed in the splendor of forms and of nature, the Middle Ages was tormented by spiritual doubts and anguish. It was gloomy and beset by nightmares: feudal power often ended up in monasteries as did beauty in nunneries. Roman corruption held no attraction even as a memory; the dissolution of the great Empire had inoculated the idea of impotence into the human spirit. It was a complete reversal: the ancient world had reduced the supernatural forces to plastic forms; the Middle Ages expanded them into infinity. The human spirit, contained in space and time, annihilated itself with Brahmanic resignation. Such a prostration stifled all initiative and inquiry. Dogma ruled over beliefs as did erudition over knowledge, discipline over customs. Through the period of Roman decadence, humanity endured its afflictions with stoic indifference and sought the pleasures of life with epicurean sensuality; in the Middle Ages man chose to escape life through ecstasy and gave rise to a new Christian mythology full of remorse, fears and prayers. Thought accepted the authority of faith, the handbook of logic formed an appendix to the catechism. Under such conditions terror prevailed and people expected the end of the world . . . At last a new world emerged with respect both to matter and spirit. It was a period of exultation and at the same time of melancholy and reflection: but it manifested itself in two distinct movements: as a cult of beauty and force—the Renaissance—among the Latins, and as free inquiry—the Reformation—among the Germanic peoples. There was an increasing number of conflicts in institutions, private lives, traditions, laws and literature. It was not an antithesis perceived by the intellect or glimpsed by imagination; it was not a struggle against human nature as in the Middle Ages; it manifested itself as a strident dissonance at all levels of thought and action: it was a conflict between the new spirit and the old forms. In this situation the triumph of either one had a decisive influence on institutions, knowledge and art. In this connection we should point out that the struggle produced different results among the Germanic and the Latin peoples—a difference that largely explains why humor developed so well among the first and not at all among the second.[5]

Now, one should first of all realize that, in dealing critically with an expression of art so peculiarly and uniquely original as

[5] Giorgio Arcoleo, *L'umorismo nell'arte moderna*. Due conferenze al Circolo filologico di Napoli (Naples: Detken, 1885), pp. 6–10.

humor, these hasty synopses and ideal historical reconstructions cannot be accepted as valid. When a legend is created, the collective imagination rejects all the elements, features and characteristics which are at variance with the ideal nature of a given action or personality and, instead, evokes and combines all the suitable images: the same thing happens when we draw a summary sketch of a given period and are inevitably led to overlook the many discordant details and specific manifestations. We are unable to hear the voices of protest in the midst of an overpowering chorus. We know that there are certain vivid colors that, if scattered here and there and looked at from a distance, will thin out, fade, and blend with the prevailing shades of blue or gray of the landscape. In order for these colors to stand out and fully re-acquire their individual brightness, we need to draw close to them. We will then realize how and to what degree we were deceived by distance.

If we accepted Taine's theory that moral phenomena are as subject to deterministic laws as physical phenomena, that human history is a part of natural history, and that the works of art are products of specific factors and specific laws (i.e., the law of dependency with the ensuing rule of the essential traits and dominant faculties, and the law of conditions and circumstances which entails the observance of such factors as the primeval forces, race, milieu, and historical moment); if we considered the works of art only as inevitable effects of natural and social forces, we would never penetrate the inner core of art. We would be compelled to see all the artistic manifestations of a given period as concordant and concomitant, each depending on the others and all of them reflecting that characteristic which, according to our superficial conception or notion, has brought them together and produced them. We would not see reality, which is infinitely varied and constantly changing, and the individual feelings and perceptions of reality, which also are infinitely varied and constantly changing. After considering the sky, the climate, the sun, the society, customs and prejudices, we have to look at each individual in order to find out what these elements have become according to the particular psychic structure, the unique, original combination of elements which makes up each individual. Where one person gives up, another rebels; where one weeps, another laughs; and there may always be someone who laughs and weeps at the same time. In the world around him, man, in this or any other period, sees only those things that interest him: from early infancy, without being aware of it in the slightest, man selects, accepts, and absorbs certain elements; later, these elements, stirred by feelings and emotions, will mix and mingle in the most varied combinations.

"Antiquity unperturbably compressed abstract forms into the harmony of the finite." Here is a generalization. All of antiquity? Is there no exception? "Either the Cyclops or the Gnome, the Graces or the Parcae." And why not also the Sirens, half woman, half fish? "Life had either free men or slaves." And couldn't a free man have felt enslaved and a slave have felt inwardly free? Doesn't Arcoleo himself quote Diogenes who "enclosed the world in a barrel and would not accept the greatness of Alexander if it obstructed his view of the sun"? And what does it mean that the Greek intellect perceived the contrast and Art was incapable of expressing it because life was different? What was life like? All tears or all laughter? How could the intellect then grasp the contrast? All abstractions are necessarily rooted in a concrete fact. What existed, therefore, was tears *and* laughter, not tears *or* laughter; and if the intellect was able to grasp the contrast, why should art have been incapable of expressing it? "At best," says Arcoleo, "the sense of contrast made its way from the sphere of the intellect to that of imagination where it became a phantasy, and this is when Aristophanes wrote his satires of the sophists and Lucian satirized the Gods." What does "at best" mean? If the sense of contrast made its way from the sphere of intellect to that of imagination where it turned into a phantasy, this means that it became art. What then? Let's leave Aristophanes out of it, for, as we shall see, he has nothing to do with humor; but Lucian was not only the author of the dialogue of the Gods. And let us proceed.

"The ancients reduced the supernatural forces to plastic forms." Here is another generalization. All of the ancient world and all of the supernatural forces? Including fate? And during the Renaissance did all Italy remain "pagan and serene in their pleasures, and had no curiosity, no intimacy"? We shall see. We are now discussing humor and its artistic manifestations which, I repeat, are extraordinary and uniquely original: only one humorist would suffice; we shall find a good many in every place and period; and we shall explain why it happens that Italian humorists particularly do not seem to us to be humorists.

All divisions are arbitrary. Shortly after the publication of Nencioni's essay (in which, as we have seen, he denied not only that the ancients had a humoristic art, but also that they could have had one), the opposite point of view was taken in Italy first by Fraccaroli and then by Bonghi and other critics, who showed that there was much more humor in classical—particularly Greek —literature than Nencioni had been able to see.[6] The "fine balance," the "dispassionate poise" and the "healthy" and "youthful" spirit, the "serene harmony" of the life and temperament of the ancients, and the fact that they depicted nature with veritable accuracy devoid of melancholy and nostalgia—all of these are old war horses of romantic criticism. Schiller himself, who was the first to create that division, had to recognize that Euripides, Horace, Propertius and Virgil did not have a simple and unsophisticated concept of nature and that consequently there were "sentimental" souls among the ancients and Greek souls among the moderns, and had to dismiss as untenable the traditional cleavage between ancient and modern inspiration.

Following the lead of Biese's *Die Entwickelung des Naturgefühls bei den Griechen,* Basch readily showed how much "sentiment" there was in Greek poetry and thought, in primitive mythology, in the often grotesque metamorphoses of the gods, in the nostalgic Golden Age utopia, in the refined melancholy of the lyric poets and particularly of the elegiac poets, who presented nature not only "as the framework for our feelings, but also as having deep and mysterious affinities with them."[7] Also Herder, who first differentiated between *Kunst-poesie* and *Natur-poesie,* did not intend this distinction to have a rigorously chronological sense. And Richter rejected the idea that Christianity had been the cause and exclusive source of the new poetry, since the Scandinavian Edda poems, as well as poems from India, originated outside the domain of Christian mysticism. Following Herder's observation that "no poet remains loyal to a single inspiration of feeling,"[8] Richter designated as romantic not the authors but the literary works inspired by feeling. Heine said in *Germania* that it was a deplorable error to define classic art as plastic, as if all art which aims at being art, ancient or modern, should not necessarily be plastic in its external form. And we don't really have to recall here the predica-

[6] Giuseppe Fraccaroli, *Per gli umoristi dell'antichità* (Verona, 1885), reviewed by R. Bonghi in *La cultura,* VII, 2 (1886), 49.

[7] Basch, p. 203. The subject of Biese's book (Kiel, 1882) has been treated in later studies.

[8] Cited in Muoni, *op. cit.* [tr.]

ment that Victor Hugo got himself into when he, while attempting to establish the famous theory of the grotesque as a basis of modern art, ran up against Vulcan, Polyphemus, Silenus, the tritons, the satyrs, the cyclopses, the sirens, the furies, the Parcae, the harpies, the Homeric Tersites, and the *dramatis personae* of the comedies of Aristophanes.

Furthermore, no one today would dream of denying that the ancients were quite aware of man's profound misery. It was clearly expressed, moreover, by philosophers and poets. But, as usual, some have resolved also to see an almost total difference in substance between ancient and modern suffering, and the claim has been made that there is a gloomy progression in human suffering, which evolves with the history of civilization itself and is based on the fact that human consciousness is increasingly more sensitive and delicate, irritable and dissatisfied. But if I am not mistaken, this was already said by Solomon in times of old: an increase in knowledge brings an increase in suffering.[9] And was Solomon, in times of old, really right? It remains to be seen. If human passions develop a mutual attraction and influence as they grow increasingly more keen and intense; if man, as it is said, is led, partly by his imagination and sensitivity, into a "process of universalization" which expands ever more rapidly and forcibly so that in one moment of affliction we seem to experience many or all afflictions, do we really suffer more because of this? No, because this increase in suffering entails a lessening in intensity. And this is precisely what motivated Leopardi's sharp observation that ancient suffering was utterly hopeless, as it usually is in nature and still is among primitive and country people, namely, a suffering that lacks the consolation of sensibility and the sweet resignation to misfortunes.[10]

Today, if we think we are unhappy, the world, in our eyes, becomes a theater of universal misery. This is because, instead of plunging headlong into our own sorrow, we spread and extend it to the universe. We pluck out the thorn and wrap ourselves in a black cloud. Boredom grows, but the pain dulls and lessens. But what about the *tedium vitae* of the contemporaries of Lucretius? And what about Timon's feeling of misanthropic dejection?

Well, let's not indulge in a useless display of examples and quotations. These questions and disquisitions are purely academic. We

9 Ecclesiastes, I, 18. [tr.]
10 Giacomo Leopardi, *Zibaldone di pensieri,* no. 77.

needn't look too far back to find the humanity of our past for it is still within us, the same as always. At most, we can admit that, due to the alleged development of sensibility and progress of civilization, those dispositions of the mind and those conditions of life which are particularly conducive to humor—to be more precise, to a *certain type* of humor—are more common: but it would be completely arbitrary to deny that the ancients had or could have had those same dispositions toward humor. Indeed Diogenes, with his cask and lantern, did not live yesterday, and in no one else are the serious and the ridiculous more closely intertwined. Are Aristophanes and Lucian exceptions as Nencioni says and Arcoleo repeats? But then Swift and Sterne are also exceptions. *All* humoristic art, we say again, is and has always been an art of exception.

As the ancients wept differently from us, say these critics, so naturally they laughed differently. Jean Paul Richter's distinction between the classical comic sense and the romantic comic sense is well known; he identifies the first with gross jestings and vulgar satire derisive of vices and defects without any commiseration or pity, and the second with humor proper, a philosophical laughter mixed with pain because it stems from the comparison between the small finite world and the infinite idea, a laughter full of tolerance and sympathy.

In Italy Leopardi, who was always nostalgic of the past and who clearly indicated that he experienced suffering not as the romantics but as the ancients did—a suffering that was desperate and hopeless—defended the comic sense of the ancients against that of the moderns.

The comic of the ancients had a real substance, which was always expressed concretely, making you feel and see the physical presence of the ridiculous. The modern comic, instead . . . is merely a shadow, a ghost, a breath, a gust of wind, a cloud of smoke. The former filled people with laughter, the latter barely affords a taste of it; the former was solid and firm, the latter is ephemeral; the former consisted of images, similarities, comparisons, stories, in short, of funny things; the latter, generally and schematically speaking, consists of words, and is produced by particular word associations, ambiguities, allusions and word play, so that if you remove those allusions and double meanings and substitute one word for another, the ridiculous will vanish. But the Greek and Latin comic sense is solid, concrete, and substantial as, for instance, when Lucian, in his *Zeus Elenkómenos,* compares the gods hanging from Fate's distaff to little fish hanging from a fisherman's pole . . . But it appears as if what was once called Attic salt—a type of wit that pleased the Greeks, the most civilized people of antiquity, and the Latins—strikes the modern and especially the French as something gross and coarse. And maybe Horace already held a similar opinion when he disapproved of Plautus' salty comedy: in fact, the comic sense in Horace's satires and epistles is not quite as concrete as that of the ancient Greeks and Latins but neither is it in any way as subtle as that of the moderns. Today, by dint of repeated jokes and witticisms, also the comic sense has become rarified and so thin and subtle that it is not even a liquid substance anymore but ether or vapor. Only this kind is today regarded as worthy of the witty people of good taste and style, and worthy of high society and refined conversation. In the old comedies the sense of the ridiculous stemmed to a large extent also from the very actions that the characters were brought out to perform on stage, and the ridiculous was still conceived in terms of pure action and the stage was not a small source of wit; take, for instance, Maffei's *Cerimonie*: a true example of the old sense of the ridiculous is when Horace enters the house through the window in order to avoid the complimentary greetings at the door. Another important difference between the ancient and the modern sense of the comic is that the former favored popular or familiar subjects or at least subjects that one does not find in the most refined conversation, which did not exist then or at least had not yet evolved to so great a degree of refinement. The modern comic sense, instead, particularly the French, deals mainly with the most exquisite world, with the things of the most refined nobility and the personal vicissitudes of the most modern families, etc.— something that, relatively speaking, may be said also of Horace's sense of the ridiculous. Thus, the comic among the ancients had solidity and lasted a long time, like the edge of a dull sword, whereas modern wit, just as it has a very sharp cutting edge, an edge with varying degrees of sharpness depending more or less upon the period and the country, so it is ruined and worn out in a split second, and it is not felt by the common people, like a fresh cut from a sharp blade.[11]

Evidently Leopardi is here speaking of the French *esprit* as opposed to the classical sense of the ridiculous, without realizing that, as Taine said, "the spirit of conversation, the talent for *faire des mots,* the taste for lively and witty phrases, unexpected, ingenious and spiced with gaiety and malice," is also classical and quite old in France: "Duas res industriosissime persequitur gens Gallorum, rem militarem et argute loqui" ("Two things the Gauls pursue most industriously, military activity and wit").[12] This *esprit* —French in origin, and which has gradually become refined and conventional, aristocratic and elegant in certain literary periods— is certainly not modern humor and much less English humor with

11 *Ibid.,* no. 41. [tr.]

12 Hippolyte Taine, "De l'esprit anglais," Chap. VIII of *Notes sur l'Angleterre* (Paris, 1903), p. 339. ["Faire des mots" is the art of making witticisms. The Latin quote is from Cato, *Hist. frg.*—tr.]

which Taine contrasts it on the basis that English humor is made
not of "words" but of "things" or, in some respect, of common
sense (if—as Joubert thought—common sense consists of useful
notions while *esprit* consists of many useless ones).[13] Let's not
confuse the two, then.

In 1899, Alberto Cantoni, a most acute Italian humorist who
was deeply affected by the conflict between reason and feeling and
who suffered for not being able to be as genuine and spontaneous
as his nature prompted him to be, resumed the subject in an
allegorized story called "Humour classico e moderno."[14] In this
story he imagines that an attractive, ruddy and jovial old man,
who represents classical humor, and a wary little man with a
mawkish and facetious expression on his face, who represents
modern humor, meet in front of the statue of Gaetano Donizetti
in Bergamo and immediately begin to quarrel. Then they propose
in the way of a challenge that, each on his own, as though they
were total strangers, they should go to Clusone, a town in the
nearby countryside where a fair is being held; then in the evening,
back again at the statue of Donizetti, they will recount and compare their fleeting and particular impressions of the trip. Instead
of discussing and analyzing the nature, purpose, and flavor of
ancient and modern humor, Cantoni relates, in a lively dialogue,
the impressions gathered by the jovial old man and the circum-
spect little man at the Clusone fair. The old man's impressions
could have been the subject of a story by Boccaccio, Firenzuola,
or Bandello; the comments and sentimental variations of the little
man sound like Sterne's *Sentimental Journey* or Heine's *Reise-
bilder*. Given his predilection for natural spontaneity, Cantoni
would side with the ruddy old man if he were not forced to
recognize that the old man has wanted to remain as he was, much
beyond what his age would tolerate, and that he is somewhat
coarse and often shamefully sensual. But Cantoni also feels and
understands the conflict that constantly splits and tears the soul
of the small and thin man, so he has the old man address him with
harsh and biting remarks:

"Because you have repeated so many times that you seem to be all smiles
on the outside but that inside you are actually all sorrow . . . , one can-

13 J. Joubert, *Pensées* (Paris, 1901), p. 50. [tr.]
14 Cantoni calls this work "grottesco," perhaps because it mixes imagination
and criticism. For a study of Cantoni's work, see L. Pirandello, "Un critico
fantastico," in *Arte e scienza* (Rome: W. Modes, 1908), [now also in *Saggi,
poesie, scritti varii*—tr.].

not tell anymore what you seem to be or what you actually are . . . If you could see yourself, you would not understand, as I don't, whether you feel more like crying or laughing."

"This is true today," Modern Humour answers, "because I now think that you stopped half way. In your time the joys and torments of life had two different forms or at least they appeared to be simpler and quite dissimilar to each other. Nothing was easier than to set them apart and then to elevate one to the detriment of the other. Then in my time came criticism, and that was the end of that. For a long time we groped in the dark wondering which was the best or the worst until the *tormenting* aspects of happiness and the *amusing* aspects of sorrow began to emerge from their long hiding. The ancients also believed that pleasure was only the cessation of pain and that pain itself, if carefully considered, was not at all to be identified with evil. But they held these nice ideas in earnest, which is like saying that they were not in the least convinced. Now, alas, my time has come and we keep saying almost laughingly—that is, with the most profound conviction—that the two elements recently associated with joy and sorrow, have faded and have become so indefinite that it is impossible even to tell them apart, not to speak of separating them. The result is that my contemporaries no longer know how to be either very happy or very unhappy, and that you alone are no longer capable of stimulating the tempered pleasure of the first or diverting the sophistic quivering fears of the second. Since I know how to mix everything, I am now needed to disperse as many deceiving mirages as possible, on one hand, and to smoothen as many superfluous rough edges as I find, on the other. I live by makeshift and by providing protective padding . . ."

"A fine life!" says the old man.

". . . in order to reach an intermediate stage which may represent, as it were, the gray substance of human sensibility. In other times people laughed too much, and free of charge; nowadays people feel too much. It is urgent however that the mind restrain the most disorderly displays of sentiment . . . While I am constantly regretting not being allowed to inherit your illusions, I am also glad to be on my side of the ditch, well trained against the snares of those illusions. But what's wrong? Why do you stare at me that way?"

"I think," says the ruddy old man, "that if you really want to have a double soul, you are right not to do like the famous widower in love . . . who wept over his dead wife with his left eye while winking at his new sweetheart with his right eye. On the other hand, you are trying to weep and wink at the same time and with both eyes, which is like saying that we can no longer make any sense of it."[15]

Like in the romantic drama that the two nice bourgeois Dupuis and Cotonet saw "dressed in black and white, laughing with one

[15] A. Cantoni, *Romanzi e racconti* (Milan, 1903), pp. 593–95. [tr.]

eye and crying with the other."[16] But here we have confusion again. Cantoni, in a different way, is saying essentially what Richter and Leopardi had said. The difference is that he calls humor what the other two had called the classical sense of the comic and of the ridiculous. Richter, a German, praises the romantic sense of the comic or modern humor and severely censures the classical sense of the comic as coarse and vulgar, whereas Cantoni, like Leopardi, as a good Italian is wont to do, defends the latter type, even though he recognizes that the charge of shameful sensuality is not at all undeserved. But Cantoni also believes that modern humor is nothing but an adulterated form of the ancient. In fact, he has Classical Humour say to Modern Humour: "Well, my idea is that it has always been possible to do without you, or that you are only the worst part of me, which is now raising its cocky head as is the custom these days. It is a true saying that one is bound never to know himself well by himself! You certainly slipped away from me and I didn't even notice it."

Now is this true? Is Cantoni's Classical Humour really humor? Or doesn't Cantoni make, from one point of view, the same mistake that Leopardi made, from another, when he confused the French *esprit* with the whole of modern humor? More precisely: what Cantoni calls Classical Humour, would it not be humor in a much wider sense, one that would include jest, mock, and wit, in short, the comic in all its varied expressions?

This is the very crux of the question. It is not a matter of the difference between ancient and modern art nor is it a matter of ethnic prerogatives. It is rather a question of whether humor should be considered in the wide sense in which it is usually and mistakenly considered, or rather in a narrower but more appropriate sense. If we take it in the wide sense, we will find a wealth of examples in both the ancient and modern literatures of all nations; if we take it in its more restricted sense, we will also find it in the ancient and modern literatures of all countries, but we will find much less of it, in fact, only very few exceptional manifestations.

[16] Alfred De Musset, "Lettres de Dupuis et Cotonet," Première Lettre, in *Oeuvres Complètes*, Vol. IX (Paris, 1866), p. 201. [tr.]

Chapter III.   SUMMARY DISTINCTIONS

As is well known, Taine attempted to compare French and English *esprit:*

It should not be said that the English are wanting in wit: they have a wit which is entirely their own; it may not be very pleasant, but it is quite original, its flavor strong, keen and even somewhat bitter like their national drinks. They call it "humour" and it generally is the wit of a man who tells a joke with a straight face. It abounds in the writings of Swift, Fielding, Sterne, Dickens, Thackeray, and Sydney Smith; in this respect, the *Book of Snobs* and *Peter Plymley's Letters* are masterpieces. A great deal that is of the most indigenous and biting quality is also found in Carlyle. It may border on clownish caricature or on deliberate sarcasm; it shakes the nerves, or it makes a lasting impression on the memory. It is a product either of a drollish imagination, or of concentrated indignation. It delights in violent contrasts, in unexpected disguises. It dresses folly in the garments of reason and reason in the garments of folly. Those who are more abundantly endowed with it outside England are Heinrich Heine, Aristophanes, Rabelais, and occasionally Montesquieu. Even so, one would have to subtract from the last three mentioned an element which is alien to the British and which, like certain types of good wine, is only grown under sunny skies, the element, that is, of French verve, joy, and gaiety. For in its pure and insular state this type of humor always leaves a sour after-taste. The man who uses it is seldom benevolent and never happy; he feels and fiercely denounces the discords of life. He doesn't really derive any pleasure from them; he deeply suffers and is irritated by them. It is a continual feeling of melancholy and anger that leads him to analyze the grotesques of life and coldly to sustain his irony. Perfect examples of this kind of humor must be sought in the great writers, but the genre is so native to England that one finds examples of it in ordinary conversation, in literature, in political debates: it is the current coin of *Punch*.[1]

The quotation is a bit too long but suitable here to clarify several things. Taine is quite successful in grasping the broad difference between the *plaisanterie*—or rather the humor—of the French and that of the British. Each people has its own sense of

[1] Hippolyte Taine, "De l'esprit anglais," *Notes sur l'Angleterre* (Paris, 1903), pp. 344–45.

humor, which has general distinctive characteristics. As usual, however, we cannot carry this too far, that is, we cannot accept those general characteristics as a solid foundation for the study of such a special art as the one we are dealing with. What would we say of a person who—on the basis of a broad survey establishing that there are certain common bodily features which, in the main, distinguish an Englishman from a Spaniard, a German from an Italian, etc.—would draw the conclusion that all Englishmen have, for instance, the same eyes, the same nose and the same mouth?

In order to understand well how generic this kind of distinction is, let us stay for a moment within the confines of Italy. Since we belong to it, we Italians can easily notice how and to what degree the physiognomy of one person differs from that of another. But while this is quite obvious to us who are natives of this country, it is extremely difficult for a foreigner to realize that we do not all look alike. Let us imagine a large forest with many families of trees: oaks, maples, beeches, planes, pines etc. At first glance, we can summarily identify the various families by the height of the trees and the varying shades of green, in short, by the general configuration of each family. But then we should consider that, within each family, each tree differs from all the other trees, each trunk, branch or shrub differs from all the other trunks, branches or shrubs; indeed, in such an immense foliage, we wouldn't even find two leaves that are identical.

Now, if it were a matter of judging a work of the collective imagination, as in the case of a genuine epic poem which emerged vividly and powerfully from the primitive traditional legends of a certain people, we could somehow accept a broad and general definition. But when dealing with individual creations, particularly if they are works of humor, we can no longer be satisfied with that type of generalization. Using abstractly the type of English humor, Taine puts Swift, Fielding, Sterne, Dickens, Thackeray, Sydney Smith and Carlyle all together, and even includes Heine, Aristophanes, Rabelais and Montesquieu as well. Now, that is quite a collection! From humor understood in the broad sense and from the typical manner that, as a common characteristic, a particular people has of expressing its humor, we make a big jump to those singular and unique humoristic expressions which can be understood in a broad sense only at the cost of completely renouncing criticism—I mean the type of criticism that examines and brings out those individual traits that distinctly separate one expression, one art, one mode of being, and one style from any other, so that we can see how Swift is different from Fielding, how Sterne is different from both Swift and Fielding, how Dickens differs from Swift, Fielding and Sterne, and so on. The relations that each of these humoristic writers may have either with the national English humor or among themselves are entirely secondary and superficial; and they are totally irrelevant with respect to esthetic valuation.

What these writers may have in common does not derive from the quality of English national humor, but rather from the sole fact that they are humorists, each in his own way and yet all authentic humorists—writers, that is, who experience that inner and peculiarly special process which results in the artistic expression that is typical of humor. For this reason alone, not only Heine, Rabelais and Montesquieu but all true humorists of every period and country can join their ranks. Not, however, Aristophanes, for in him that process does not take place. In Aristophanes we do not really have contrast but only opposition. He is never caught in a dilemma. He sees only his reasons and is always stubbornly *against*—against all innovation, that is, against rhetoric, which fosters demagoguery, against the new music which, changing the old and sanctioned modes, poses a constant threat to the foundations of education and of the State, against the tragedies of Euripides which unnerve the moral temper and corrupt the customs, against the philosophy of Socrates which can only produce unruly spirits and atheists, etc. Some of his comedies are like fables written by a fox in response to the fables which men have written slandering the animals. In the comedies of Aristophanes men reason and act with the logic of animals, while in the fables the animals reason and act with the logic of men. They are allegories in a fantastic drama, in which the jesting is a hyperbolic, merciless satire.[2] Aristophanes has a moral purpose and consequently his world is never one of pure fantasy. He has no interest in verisimilitude; he doesn't pay any attention to it because he is constantly referring to real things and real people; he makes hyperbolic abstractions out of contingent reality but does not create a fantastic reality, as does Swift, for instance. Aristophanes is not a humorist, but Socrates is, as Theodor Lipps acutely observed:

[2] See Jacques Denis, *La comédie grecque,* vol. I (Paris: Hachette, 1886), Chap. VI, and Ettore Romagnoli's fine and learned preface to his translations of Aristophanes' comedies (Turin: Bocca, 1908).

Socrates attends the performance of the *Clouds* and laughs with the others at the mockery which the poet makes of him. Socrates understands the viewpoint of popular consciousness, which Aristophanes has chosen to represent, and sees in it something relatively good and judicious. He even recognizes the relative right of those who deride his fight against popular consciousness and it is only because of this recognition that his laughter comes to share in the laughter of the others. On the other hand, he still laughs at those who laugh; he does this and can do it because he is aware of the higher right and inevitable victory of his own views. It is precisely this sense of certainty that shines through his laughter and makes it appear logically plausible and justifiable even in its folly, and morally superior even in its nothingness.[3]

Socrates has the *feeling of the opposite*. Aristophanes could at best be considered a humorist only if we take humor in the broad but erroneous sense which comprises jest, mock, wit, satire, caricature, in short, all the numerous and varied expressions of the comic. But if we understand humor in this sense, then many more other burlesque, witty, grotesque, satiric and comic writers of every country and period should also be regarded as humorists.

It is always the same mistake, that of drawing general distinctions. No one can deny that all countries have different qualities and that the French *plaisanterie* is not the same as the English kind or the Italian, the Spanish, the German, the Russian kind, and so on. No one can deny that each people has its own kind of humor. The error begins when this humor, naturally variable in its manifestations according to the historical moment and the milieu, is considered, as the common people usually consider it, as true humor; or when, because of external and general considerations, it is found that the humor of the ancients is substantially different from that of the moderns; and finally when, because of the mere fact that the English gave the name *humour* to their national humor while other people called it something else, it is concluded that only the English have true humor.

We have already seen that, long before Swift, Addison, Fielding, Sterne and the other writers of that 18th century group called themselves humorists, Italy had the *umidi, umorosi* and *umoristi*.[4] This is with respect to the word humor. But if we want to talk about the thing itself, we have to consider that, should we take

[3] Theodor Lipps, *Komik und Humor: Eine psychologisch-aesthetishe Untersuchung* (Hamburg and Leipzig: Voss, 1898), p. 239.
[4] See W. M. Thackeray, *The English Humourists of the Eighteenth Century* (Leipzig: Tauchnitz, 1853). In addition to the writers mentioned, the group included Congreve, Steele, Prior, Gay, Pope, Hogarth, Smollett, and Goldsmith.

humor in its broader definition, all the numerous writers we identify as burlesque, ironic, satiric, comic, etc., would be called humorists by the English, who would perceive in them that special flavor which we perceive in their writers and never in ours because, as Pascoli very aptly explained,

Every language and literature has a special and untranslatable *quid,* something that can be easily perceived by a foreigner but that only few people are able to sense in their own language and literature. Foreign languages, even the ones we do not understand, fall on our ear, say, more wondrously than our own. A foreign story or poem, however mediocre, will seem more beautiful than many beautiful things of our own; and the more so, the greater the national quiddity they comprise. Naturally, then, our language and literature will have the same effect on other people as the foreign languages have on us.[5]

A proof of this can be seen in a statement by William Roscoe, an Englishman who was well aware of what humor is commonly understood to be in his country, on the jocose compositions of Berni, Bini and Mauro: "That these early productions led the way to a similar eccentricity of style in other countries is not improbable, and perhaps the most characteristic idea of the writings of Berni and his associates may be obtained by considering them to be, in lively and unaffected verse, what the works of Rabelais, of Cervantes, and of Sterne, are in prose."[6] And what about the following definition of Berni's style written by Antonio Panizzi, who lived for a long time in England and wrote in English on Italian literature:

The ingenuity with which he finds a resemblance between distant objects, and the rapidity with which he suddenly connects the most remote ideas; the solemn manner in which he either alludes to ludicrous events, or utters an absurdity; the air of innocence and naïveté with which he presents remarks full of shrewdness and knowledge of the world; that peculiar *bonhommie* with which he seems to look kindly and at the same time unwillingly on human errors or wickedness; the keen irony which he uses with so much appearance of simplicity and aversion to bitterness; the seeming singleness of heart with which he appears anxious to excuse men and actions, the very moment he is most inveterate in exposing them; these are the chief elements of Berni's poetry.[7]

[5] Giovanni Pascoli, *Prose,* 2nd ed. (Milan: Mondadori, 1952), I, 517. [tr.]

[6] William Roscoe, *The Life and Pontificate of Leo the Tenth* (London, 1846), p. 130.

[7] Boiardo, *Orlando innamorato,* Ariosto, *Orlando furioso,* ed. Antonio Panizzi, with an essay on the Romantic narrative poetry of the Italians; 5 vols. (London: Pickering, 1830), II, pp. cxix–cxx. [tr.]

Does not this correspond, to a large extent, to Nencioni's later definition that humor "is a natural bent of heart and mind toward empathic and indulgent observation of the contradictions and absurdities of life"? At any rate, it is evident that Roscoe perceived in Berni and the other jocose poets of Italy the same flavor he perceived in the English writers who were endowed with humor. And did not Byron perhaps sense it in our Pulci and even to the extent of translating the first canto of his *Morgante*? And did not Sterne perceive it in Gian Carlo Passeroni (that "Passeroni dabben," as Parini called him), that good priest from Nice who alludes to *The Life and Opinions of Tristram Shandy* when he tells us:

E già mi disse un chiaro letterato
inglese, che da questa mia stampita
il disegno, il modello avea cavato
di scrivere in piú tomi la sua vita
e pien di gratitudine e d'amore
mi chiamava suo duce e precettore.[8]

(A famous English man of letters
once told me that from this little publication of mine
he has taken the plan, the model
for a story of his life in several volumes;
full of gratitude and love,
he calls me his guide and teacher.)

On the other hand, is that group of English humorists we have just mentioned really free from the influence by French writers of the *grand siècle* and other periods? Voltaire, speaking of Swift in his letters on the English, wrote: "Mr. Swift is Rabelais in his senses and while living in good company. Indeed, he does not have the gaiety of his predecessor, but he has all the subtlety, reason, discrimination, good taste which our rural vicar of Meudon lacks. His verse is of a singular and almost inimitable taste. True humor, whether in prose or in verse, seems to be his special talent. Yet, to understand him well, one must take a short trip to his country."[9]

To his country—granted; but there are also those who claim that one should likewise take a trip to the moon in the company of Cyrano de Bergerac.

And who will question the effect of Voltaire and Boileau on

---

[8] Gian Carlo Passeroni, *Cicerone*, Pt. III, Canto XVII, 122.

[9] Voltaire, *Lettres sur les Anglais*, 22. Voltaire's praise of an English writer compared with a French writer sounds quite odd after reading Taine's remarks on English and French *esprit*.

Pope? We need only recall that Lessing, attacking Gottsched in his letters on modern literature, said that imitation of the English—Shakespeare, Jonson, Beaumont, Fletcher—would have been more fitting and profitable to the German taste and tradition than the imitation of the "frenchified" Addison.[10]

But an even clearer proof can be drawn from the fact that not one of the Italian students of humor—who are snobbishly prejudiced in limiting its existence to England—has ever dreamed of calling Boccaccio a humorist for his many stories filled with laughter; instead, Chaucer is held to be a humorist, indeed the first of all humorists, for his *Canterbury Tales*. In the work of the English poet they chose not to see—as they should have seen—the special *quid* of his different language, a different style; instead, they chose to see a greater intimate quality in his style and to evidence this quality first of all by the ingenious pretext of the tales (the pilgrimage to Canterbury), by the portraits of the pilgrim-storytellers (particularly the unforgettable and charming Prioress Elgantine, Sir Thopas, and the good Wife of Bath), and finally by the harmonious correspondence of the tales to the character of the narrators, that is, by the manner in which the various tales, which are not invented by Chaucer, gain their color and quality from the pilgrims who narrate them.

But this observation, seemingly profound, is actually a most superficial one for it focuses only on the frame of the picture. Can the magnificent opulence of Boccaccio's style, the abundance and ostensibility of the form, be considered as mere externals, on one hand, and imply a scarcity of psychological depth, on the other? Let us examine from this point of view each individual story, the individual characters, the development of passions, the detailed, distinctly clear and evident depiction of reality which implies an extremely subtle analysis, a profound understanding of the human heart, and we shall find Boccaccio to surpass Chaucer by far, especially in the art of giving credibility to certain excessively strange adventures.

Too much attention has been paid to an observation—as usual, one of summary and general nature—made by those who have studied with excessive love for foreign things the relations between Italian and other literatures: the observation, that is, that Italian writers have always given a "greater external beauty," a more

---

[10] Gotthold Lessing, *Briefe, die neueste Literatur Betreffend,* no. 17.

sedate and harmonious linear form to all that they have borrowed from the outside, whereas foreign writers have given a greater internal beauty and a more intimate and profound character to everything they borrowed from the Italian. Now this observation, if ever true, may be applied to certain mediocre writers from whom some great foreign author has taken topics and ideas as, for instance, in the case of certain short story writers from whom Shakespeare drew the plots for some of his powerful dramas. But it is not valid for Boccaccio and Chaucer. What is needed in this case, assuming that Chaucer did not take anything directly from Boccaccio, is to consider what a skeleton-like French *fabliau* has become in the stories of each of the two writers.

Chapter IV. HUMOR AND RHETORIC

In his book *Dal Rinascimento al Risorgimento,* Giacomo Barzellotti—following Taine's precepts as well as some ideas expressed by Bonghi in his *Lettere critiche* and by an ethological study of the inter-dependence between the moral and social traits of the Italians, their way of thinking, congenital instincts and particular aptitude for conceiving and expressing beauty, and taking up the problem of sincerity in art and style in Italian literature—stated that one of all the Italian prejudices is "to presuppose that the art of writing is exclusively or primarily the craft of external form and style. While the study of form and style is indeed an essential requirement for writing, they are first and foremost *a work of inner thought,* that is, something that can be achieved if it is accepted immediately and as an end in itself, something that can only be arrived at from some other point, that is, not from the word itself but from the inside, from thought, study, meditation, and from the profound elaboration of the idea and subject matter."[1]

Now, as we know, the prejudice Barzellotti refers to is that of Rhetoric, which was an intellectualistic poetics founded solely on abstractions and logic, and it in fact was defined as the counterpart of logic.[2] According to Rhetoric, art was an activity that had to obey certain principles, which were universal and absolute as if the work of art were a statement to be formulated like a logical argument. Rhetoric said: 'This is the way it was done; this is the way it must be done.' Rhetoric collected numerous models of unchanging beauty as in a museum and required that they be imitated. Rhetoric and imitation are essentially the same thing.

And unquestionably, the damages it caused to literature in every period are, as everyone knows, incalculable. Founded on the prejudice of the so called "tradition," Rhetoric taught writers to

---

[1] Giacomo Barzellotti, *Dal Rinascimento al Risorgimento* (Palermo: Sandron, 1904), p. 198.

[2] Cf. Aristotle, *Rhetoric* I, 1.

imitate that which is inimitable: style, character, form. It did not understand that each form must be neither ancient nor modern but unique and inalienable, for it can belong to only one work of art, and that therefore no tradition can or should exist in art.

Controlled as it was by reason, Rhetoric perceived categories everywhere and saw literature as a kind of filing cabinet: for each compartment, a label. So many categories, so many corresponding genres; and each genre had its predetermined and inalterable form. It is true that Rhetoric often adjusted, but to yield, never. Whenever a rebel poet gave the filing cabinet a well-aimed kick and created a new form of his own, the rhetoricians would growl at him for quite a while. Eventually, however, if the new form succeeded in obtaining recognition, they would then take it, disassemble it like a little machine, give it a logical formulation and catalogue it, perhaps by adding a new box to the file. This is what happened, for instance, with the historical drama of that barbarian, Shakespeare. Did Rhetoric give up? No; after growling for quite some time, it admitted historical drama to its ranks and prescribed the rules for it. But it is also true that whenever the dogs of Rhetoric got hold of a poor poet whose mind had become feeble, they would tear him to pieces and force him to mistreat his own work in which he had neglected to follow strictly the model imposed upon him. An example: Tasso's *Gerusalemme conquistata*.

Culture, as viewed by Rhetoric, was not preparing the soil, spading, plowing, hoeing, fertilizing, so that the fertile seed, the vital pollen, which a favorable wind was to drop at the right time, could sprout healthy roots, and find in that soil plenty of nourishment and grow strong and solid and effortlessly, tall and powerful in its yearning for the sun. No; culture for Rhetoric consisted in the planting of poles and dressing them with branches. Preserved in their glass-house, the old trees lost their green and withered; and with the dead foliage, yellowed leaves and dried flowers Rhetoric taught how to dress up trunks of ideas not rooted in life.

For Rhetoric, thought originated first, then came form; that is, it was not like Minerva dressed in armor as she issued forth from Jupiter's head. Thought was born all naked, the poor thing, and Rhetoric dressed it. The garment was the form.

Rhetoric, in short, was like a wardrobe, the wardrobe of eloquence to which naked thoughts went to get dressed. The clothes in that wardrobe were all ready to wear, all cut on old models, more or less adorned, made with humble, common, or magnificent cloth, divided into so many compartments, nicely hung and placed in the care of a wardrobe lady whose name was Convenience. She would prescribe the most appropriate clothes for the naked thoughts that went to her. 'You'd like to be an Idyll? A graceful Idyll, neat and tidy? Well, then, let me hear how you sigh: *Alas, poor me!* Excellent. Have you read Teocritus, Moschus, Bion, and Virgil's *Bucolics*? Yes? Then recite some of it, nicely. You are a nice parrot, well trained. Come here.' Then Rhetoric would open the door labeled *Idylls* and would take out a cute little shepherd's suit. 'And you, you want to be a Tragedy? A real Tragedy? It will be difficult, I warn you. You have got to be solemn and light-footed at the same time, my dear. Twenty-four hours—that's all you have. And please stay put; choose your place and stay there. Unities, you must respect the unities. You know that? Fine. But tell me something: have you the blue blood of a prince in your veins? Have you studied Aeschylus, Sophocles, and Euripides? And what about the good Seneca? Very well. And would you like to kill your children, like Medea, your husband, like Clytemnestra, or your mother, like Orestes? You want to kill a tyrant, like Brutus. I see. Come here then.' Thus thoughts were like mannequins dressed with the apparel of form. That is, form was not properly form but *formation:* it was not *born*, it was *made*. By following predetermined rules, it was composed externally, like an object. Therefore it was artifice, not art; a copy, not creation.

Now it was undoubtedly Rhetoric that caused the lack of depth evident in so many works of Italian literature; and, to limit ourselves to our particular study, it was because of Rhetoric that a good number of Italian writers, who would have had and in fact did have, as attested by much evidence, a most particular inclination toward humor, were unable to give it artistic expression precisely because they had to follow the rules of artistic composition.

As we shall see, the inner and peculiarly essential process of humor is one that inevitably *dismantles,* splits and disrupts, whereas art as taught in the schools by Rhetoric was primarily external composition, a logically ordered concordance.[3] It is obvious

[3] In a review of the first edition of the present essay published in *La Critica*, VII (1909), Croce chose to infer that, by stating that art composes while humor decomposes, I was implying that humor is the opposite of art. Now I ask any intelligent reader whether my statement warrants and justifies such a drastic and absolute deduction; and whether it is right and justifiable that, after indulging in such rash and unfounded speculation, Croce should go on

in fact—and this applies both to true humorists and to those who call themselves such—that Italian writers are either folk writers (or favor a popular style, independent of any school), or they are in open revolt against Rhetoric, that is, against the external rules of traditional literary education. One can also see that when this traditional education was disrupted, when the yoke of the classical intellectualistic poetics was overcome by the eruption of the feelings and the will which characterizes the romantic movement, those writers who had a natural disposition for humor expressed it in their work, not through imitation, but spontaneously.

In his study of Cecco Angiolieri mentioned at the beginning of this essay, Alessandro D'Ancona saw the character of true humor in the work of that bizarre thirteenth century poet. Now this is really unacceptable. Angiolieri's example can be useful in clarifying only what we just mentioned and nothing else. As I have shown elsewhere, Angiolieri's work is lacking in both the characteristics of true humor and in those characteristics that D'Ancona believes to be the traits of true humor.[4] The term melancholy, for instance, has lost the original meaning it had for Cicero and Pliny, but it is still far from conveying that delicate affection or

to say that "it is however probable that he allowed himself to say more than he wanted to, but that what he really meant to say is not that humor is not art but rather that it is a genre of art essentially distinct from all other genres taken individually and as a group." I shall return to this later in my discussion of the special activity of reflection in the conception of a work of humor. Right now I shall be satisfied to reply that Croce confuses—I don't know whether deliberately or not—the so-called "literary genres" as understood by Rhetoric (and these, we agree, should be eliminated) with those distinctions in art that are both valid and necessary if we are to avoid confusing one work of art with another and thus abolish all criticism. Croce confuses the genres with those distinctions only to conclude philosophically that all of them are art and that each of them, as art, cannot be distinguished from the others. Humor is not a "literary genre" like *poem, comedy, novel, short story,* and so on; in fact, any of these literary compositions may or may not be humoristic. Humor is a particular kind of artistic expression whose existence cannot be denied merely because all expression is art and therefore not distinguishable from all remaining art. Croce's vast preparation in philosophy (mine, you know, is very little) has led him to such an edifying conclusion. Croce has no objection to speaking individually of one humorist or another; but as soon as one tries to speak of humor in general, then his philosophy becomes a formidable, unshakeable iron gate. No admittance. But what's behind that gate? Nothing—only the equation: intuition = expression, and the assertion that it is impossible to distinguish between what is art and what is not and between artistic intuition and common intuition. Well then, don't you think we can simply go by that closed gate without even turning to look at it?

[4] L. Pirandello, "I sonetti di Cecco Angiolieri," in *Arte e scienza* (Rome: W. Modes, 1908), [now also in *Saggi, poesie, scritti varii*—tr.].

feeling which the moderns attribute to it. Melancholy for Cecco always means lack of money to squander and not having Becchina at his disposal, and waiting in vain for the old and rich father to die,

ed e' morrà quando 'l mar sarà sicco;
sí l'ha Dio fatto, per mio strazio, sano! (*Rime*, LVIII)

(and he will die when the ocean has dried up,
so hale and hearty God made him, much to my distress!).

The line, "con gran malinconia sempre i' sto" (XCVI, 1), which D'Ancona calls sobbing and which is the last instance he cites to conclude that all of Cecco's efforts to be free of melancholy are in vain, does not have the condensed value nor the expressive connotation that D'Ancona attributes to it. The contrast, that which *seems laughter and is pain,* is never to be found in Cecco. To prove that Cecco has it, D'Ancona quotes two lines out of context and gives them a meaning that they do not have:

Però malinconia non prenderaggio
anzi m'allegrerò del mi' tormento. (XCVII)

(Therefore I shall not bcome melancholy
but shall instead rejoice from my torment.)

In fact these lines are followed by a tercet which not only explains the apparent contrast, but clearly destroys it. In it Cecco says that he will not be melancholy but will instead rejoice in his torment because he has heard a wise man say that "a day will come that is worth more than a hundred"(XCVII)—the day when his father will die and he will be able to have a jolly time (*far gavezze*) as he alludes in another of his sonnets:

Sed i' credesse vivar un dí solo
piú di colui che mi fa vivar tristo,
assa' di volte ringraziere' Cristo. (LXXVII)

(If I thought I would live one day
longer than the one that makes me live miserably,
I would thank Christ many times.)

It is a day than cannot fail to come and one must await patiently:

L'uom non può sua ventura prolungare
né far piú brieve ch'ordinato sia;
ond'i' mi credo tener questa via,
di lasciar la natura lavorare

e di guardarmi, s'io 'l potrò fare,
che non m'accolga piú malinconia:
ch'i' posso dir che per la mia follia
i' ho perduto assai buon sollazzare.

Anche che troppo tardi me n'avveggio,
non lascerò ch' i' non prenda conforto,
c'a far d'un danno due sarebbe peggio.

Ond'i' m'allegro e aspetto buon porto;
ta' cose nascer ciascun giorno veggio,
che 'n dí di vita mia non mi sconforto. (IC)

(Man cannot prolong his destiny
nor can he shorten it more than it is written;
for I believe I should live like this:
to let nature work
and, if I can, to see to it
that I never feel melancholy again,
since I can say that because of my madness
I let slip by many a good time.
Although I have come to realize it too late,
I will not allow myself not to enjoy life,
for to make two ills of one would be worse.
So I cheer up and wait for a safe port;
I see such things happen every day
that, as long as I am alive, I do not lose hope.)

On the meaning of the word melancholy, which is repeatedly used
by Cecco, it is impossible to delude ourselves as D'Ancona does.
Cecco never really *rejoices* in his *torment,* but rather dresses it
in a witty and lively form which, in my opinion, often originates
from its native character, rather than from a burlesque or satiric
intention, and is entirely a popular expression of the Sienese.

Still today the Tuscans, who deservedly consider themselves the
wittiest of Italy, would not use a different form to tell about their
ill-fortune and affliction, to express their feelings of hate and love,
to manifest their indignation, reproach, and desire. Generally, to
give a comic coloring to the sentence is an innate spontaneous
virtue of the people. Belli, for instance, refused to translate the
gospel of St. Matthew into Roman dialect for Luigi L. Bonaparte
because the speech of the populace is "buffoonish" and "would
merely succeed in doing irreverence to the sacred text."[5] In short,
what we have here is not humor but irony, that is, a fictitious

---

[5] See Morandi's preface to *I sonetti romaneschi del Belli* (Città di Castello:
Lapi, 1889), Vol. I.

contradiction between what one says and what one means. The contrast is not in the feeling but is merely verbal.

If we want to include Cecco among the humorists, we have to take into account, on one hand, this general humor of the people, this clownish speech of the populace, and, on the other, humor in the wide and incorrect meaning we have discussed before. But then all other Tuscan poets should also be included for they were poets who did not belong to any school but came from the people; poets who, though not fully accomplished in art, were endowed with great spontaneity and felt the awakening spirit of human poetry either through a sweetly cherished predilection or because of true events and real feelings—and this among the puns and word-play of the followers and imitators of the Provenzal school and amid the insipid and depressing mimicry of those who wrote for the sake of distraction, fun, fashion, or gallantry· poets, in short, whose poetry announces, to put it with Bartoli, the realistic character which Italian letters will take on.

These are Tuscan poets and Tuscany is especially where we shall find expressions of humor in the broad sense; both in Tuscany and in the not at all scarce Italian literature in dialect. Why? Because humor requires above all an intimacy of style which in Italian literature has always been hindered by preoccupation over form and by all the rhetorical questions concerning language. Humor needs a highly spirited, free, spontaneous, and direct movement of language—a movement that can be achieved only when form creates itself anew each time. Now Rhetoric taught the writer not to *create* form but to *imitate* it, to compose it externally. It taught the writer to seek language from the outside as an object and naturally this type of language could only be found in books, in those books that rhetoric itself had imposed as models and as texts. What movement could one give to this external language, fixed and mummified, to this form not created anew each time but imitated, studied, and composed?

Movement is only in living language and in form that creates itself. And the humor that cannot do without this movement, I repeat, we shall find it (both in its broad sense and in its proper sense) in the humoristic expressions in dialect, in macaronic poetry, and in the writers who rebelled against Rhetoric.

Do we need to elaborate on this *creation* of form, that is, on the relationships between language and style? Schleiermacher keenly observed that the artist uses tools that by their very nature are not made for the individual but for the universal expression: such is language.[6] It is the poet who must draw from language the individual form, that is, style. Language is knowledge, objectification; style is subjectivizing this objectification. In this sense, style is *creation* of form, i.e., is the hollow word being invested and animated, in us, by a particular feeling and moved by a particular will of ours. Therefore, it is not a matter of creating *ex nihilo,* for fantasy does not create in the strict sense of the word, that is, it does not produce forms that are genuinely new. In fact, even the most capricious arabesques and the strangest grotesques—centaurs, sphinxes, winged monsters—will always reveal images that relate to real perceptions, even though they are more or less altered through various combinations.

Now, the art of language has a form that in a certain sense corresponds to the grotesque in the figurative arts—and this is in fact macaronic style, an arbitrary creation, a monstrous contamination of various elements of the cognitive world. And we note that this style originated precisely as a mode of rebellion and derision, and it was not alone but in the company of other burlesque and fictitious languages. In his introduction to *I precursori di Merlin Cocai,* Giovanni Zannoni observed:

Scorned and under-valued, dialect reacted by shrewdly infiltrating the Latin of the learned people in order to slur and slander it; thus, what had been a partial element of popular and goliardic satire became the foremost element of the new style. It showed its own flexibility while the vulgar tongue—still academic, grave, and awkward—could not adapt to all the demands of humor. It suddenly created a new mode of mocking laughter. Thus macaronic style, originating from two opposite sources, proved to be the biggest and loudest laughter of the Renaissance, the most biting barb of classicism. And yet, though unwittingly, it contributed to the final triumph of the vulgar tongue.[7]

But how many were these rebel writers, a few or many? They were only a few, for the majority is always made up of the mediocre, the *servum pecus.* Barzellotti recognizes that "a great impulse of originality and genial spontaneity" occurred "in the mind and life of the Italians during the thirteenth and fourteenth centuries." He considers this to be both the first and the true Renaissance, "for then all or nearly all the *humanists* interrupted

---

[6] Friedrich E. D. Schleiermacher, *Vorlesungen über die Aesthetik,* in *Werke,* Vol. IV (Leipzig, 1911).

[7] Giovanni Zannoni, *I precursori di Merlin Cocai* (Città di Castello, 1888), p. 12.

this original and spontaneous spark through the imitation and repetition of the ancients."[8] Now this seems another of those summary generalizations we deplored earlier and one which is akin to other similar statements concerning the great Italian Renaissance and its alleged "skeptical indifference," "pagan serenity," "mortification of individual energies," "lack of aspirations," "repose in the forms and in the senses," etc., as if the cult of antiquity were not in itself a great ideal, so great as to enlighten the world, the recovery of a heritage which was wisely employed to produce immortal works; and as if the Renaissance had not come at the right time to fill the gap created by falling or fallen ideals; as if, beside a few dry and hollow men of erudition, the Renaissance did not have many other scholars full of life and daring, their Latin pulsating and vibrating with all the energy of the Italian tongue; as if Poggio's *Facetiarum libellus unicus* was not teeming with a new spirit;[9] as if Valla had only written *Elegantiarum latinae linguae;* and finally as if Pontano, Poliziano, and many others did not have a full and fresh sense of reality which would show itself in Poliziano's vernacular writings with all the ingenuous elegance of a popular folk poet. Furthermore, beneath the world of the learned, which is so summarily and superficially understood, was there not the world of the people? And can we really say, on the other hand, that all the Italian chivalric poets did was to give the traditional subject matter a new and greater external beauty, a more composed and harmonious form? How could we speak only of external beauty if they thoroughly recreated chivalric poetry with their fantasy?

It has been too often and too lightly repeated that in the Italian temperament the intellect prevails over feeling and will, the objective over the subjective, and that this trait accounts for the fact that Italian art is more intellectualistic than sentimental, more external than internal. This inaccuracy stems from ignorance of the process of the creative activity of the spirit that we call fantasy, and such ignorance is an essential aspect of Rhetoric. The artist must feel his work as—so to speak—it feels itself, and must want it as it wants itself. To have an outer purpose and an external will

8 Barzellotti, *op. cit.*, pp. 211–213. [tr.]

9 How many sparks of true humor in Poggio! One needs only mention the story of that good man who made a deal with the minstrel to defer Hector's death, which so much distressed him; and the answer that the Spanish cardinal gave to the papal soldiers: "I am not yet hungry"; and the bandit who despaired because of a drop of milk stuck in his throat during Lent, etc.

means to go beyond the limits of art, as is in fact the case with all those who insistingly repeat that Italian Renaissance art was splendid on the outside and empty on the inside. Do we have to take empty to mean that it did not have a will and a purpose beyond itself? If so, this was a merit and not a defect. If not, then we would have to prove that it was false and artificial. Can we prove this? Yes, certainly, if we take the mediocre writers, the slaves of Rhetoric, which did in fact teach artifice and imitation. But why should we take the mediocre? Why should we settle for a broad overview in the manner of Taine without drawing distinctions? Could we ever call false the art of Ariosto?

As we set aside this group of the mediocre and prepare to face the real poets, we will realize at once that we are dealing with a question of content and not form, a question which is therefore alien to art. But this content, which we so scornfully disregard, how was it adopted by the true poets, by those who undeniably had style and therefore originality and depth of feeling? Isn't there anything that can fill the vacuum we are determined to see in them? How about their use of irony? Why do we refuse to recognize the positive implications of this irony? *Itali rident:* true, but it was a laughter that banished the Middle Ages, and how full of bile it was underneath! Was this laughter really different from Erasmus' and Ulrich of Hutten's? Why do we recognize this positive value of irony in foreign writers and deny it only to the Italians? Why do we see it in Rabelais and refuse to recognize it in Pulci and Folengo? Is it perhaps because the former was clever enough to invite his readers to do like the dog with the bone, while the latter did not? "Did you ever see a dog come across a juicy bone? He is, as Plato says (*Rep.*, II), the most philosophical of all beasts. If you have seen him, you may have noticed how devotedly and cautiously he keeps it under a watchful eye, how fervently he holds it, how carefully he takes his first bite, with what affection he breaks it, and how diligently he sucks it. What makes him do this? What is the aim of his concentrated study? What does he expect to get from it? Nothing more than a little marrow."[10]

And the bone Rabelais threw to the critics has in fact been eyed with devotion, taken cautiously and held fervently, carefully gnawed, affectionately broken, and diligently sucked. And why not

[10] Rabelais, Author's Prologue to *Gargantua and Pantagruel.* [tr.]

those of Pulci and Folengo?[11] Is it really necessary, whenever we throw a bone to the critics, to warn them that it's good and juicy? Or is it necessary to have the marrow be showing a little from one side of the bone? But with works of art, the more the will and aim have been assimilated into the artistic creation, the greater the value of those works. This greater assimilation runs the risk of being taken for indifference toward the ideals of life by those who judge with criteria alien to art and evaluate works of art superficially; but even if we overlook the fact that the ideals of life, taken in themselves, have nothing to do with art (which must be a spontaneous and independent creation), we still cannot accuse the poet of indifference because, if we do, we implicitly rule out irony: if irony is present so as to be undeniable, then the much-discussed indifference does not exist.

Rather, it should be noted that this irony rarely reaches the comic dramatization that it does with true humorists; it almost always remains undramatically comic, and is therefore mere wit, jest, and more or less grotesque caricature. The same can be said of Rabelais:

Mieulx est de ris des larmes escripre:
pour ce que rire est le propre de l'homme.[12]

(It is better to write of laughter than tears:
for laughing is natural to man.)

And Alcofribas Nasier "is condemned in the Sorbonne for the gross jests which characterize his book." What difference is there really between this gross way of jesting and that of Pulci, Folengo and Berni? Let us re-read, from this standpoint, Pulci's *Morgante maggiore* and Folengo's *Baldus,* and then Rabelais' *La vie de Gargantua* and *Les faits et le dits héroïques du bon Pantagruel roi des Dipsodes,* and we will be struck by the undeniable spiritual affinity and the undeniable derivations at every turn of the page.

And let's re-read Berni. Putting aside even the eighteen stanzas at the beginning of canto XX of his *Rifacimento* of the *Orlando innamorato* and Vergerio's booklet on Berni's Protestantism as well as all the other philosophical, social and political reflections

[11] See A. Momigliano's *L'indole e il riso di Luigi Pulci* (Rocca san Casciano: Cappelli, 1907), with which however I largely disagree as I shall say later. On Teofilo Folengo, see De Sanctis' *Storia della letteratura italiana,* Canello's *Cinquecento,* and the other studies by Zumbini and Zannoni.

[12] Rabelais, "To his readers." [tr.]

scattered throughout the *Rifacimento* itself; setting aside also his *Dialogo contro i poeti* and parodies of Petrarch which mock the *petrarchisti;* and overlooking the famous invective, *Nel tempo che fu fatto papa Adriano VI,* and the sonnets against Clemente VII: "Il papa non fa altro che mangiare,/ il papa non fa altro che dormire" ("The pope does nothing but eat/the pope does nothing but sleep"), and all other sonnets against priests and abbots, including

Poiché da voi, signor, m'è pur vietato,
che dir le vere mie ragion non possa,
per consumarmi le midolle e l'ossa
con questo nuovo strazio e non usato

(Because, my lord, you do forbid me
to confess my real reasons
why I am consumed to the bone
with this strange new torment);[13]

and not considering the chapter in praise of Aristotle (who "does not put on the Tuscan accent") and dedicated to Mr. Pietro Buffetto, a cook—setting aside all this, let us instead glean through his letters and those "chapters" that seem the most frivolous. Here is what he writes to Latino Juvenale:

Now Valerio reproachingly says that I would be better to stop the jesting and turn my mind to a better occupation. Be he damned together with those who feel as he does. What kind of penance and punishment is one that requires that I explain to the world that it is not a matter of choice but rather of misfortune? I didn't go out shopping for this torment nor did I seek it in order to make other people laugh at my life; therefore, let nobody laugh about it but the fools.

And to Monsignor Cornaro he writes: "But nature and fortune have made me such as I am, I say, not given to words nor one to stand much on ceremony, and for relief, I get entangled in the service of others." In another letter he confesses: "Driven by the fury of my suffering, I turn to poetry as a remedy." In another poem, he says that he operates "by turns of mind," and he writes to Agnolo Divizio: "consequently I work and carry out my activities day by day: What does one get out of this world but to be contented or at least *to try* to be contented?"

---

[13] XIV in F. Berni, *Poesie e prose*, ed. E. Chiòrboli (Geneva-Florence, 1934). [tr.] Cf. what Arturo Graf says on the conditions of the 16th century man of letters in his excellent *Attraverso il Cinquecento* (Turin, Florence, and Rome: Loescher, 1888).

Ciascun faccia secondo il suo cervello,
ché non siam tutti d'una fantasia.[14]

(Let each man do according to what he thinks,
for we do not all have the same mood and temper.)

And to Giovan Francesco Bini he writes: "Nevertheless I am still
a stoic like you and let this river flow toward the sea." In the
middle of the plague, he wrote to the same Divizio, then his lord,
who was running from one place to another out of fear: "Being a
man, indeed I care for life, but I have also enough of God's grace
that at the right time and place I know how not to care about it
—which is also being a man. So don't call me a coward for I am
rather worthy of being called fearless." And stoically did he behave in the middle of the plague, overcoming the fear of it and
acquiring that special feeling that is, as we shall see, essential to
humor, namely the *feeling of the opposite*. In the two "chapters"
in praise of the plague, irony successfully reaches a comic dramatization beyond wit, jest, and sheer laughter. Berni, as later Don
Abbondio, sees the scourge of the plague as a broom, but in quite
a different context of philosophical reflections:

Non fu mai malattia senza ricetta;
la natura l'ha fatte tutt'e due:
ella imbratta le cose, ella le netta. (LII)

(There was never a disease without its remedy;
nature has provided both:
she dirties things, she cleans them up.)

In fact nature, after creating ears and bells, darkness and candles,
created also the plague because "it was needed," and it was needed
because

. . . a questo corpaccio del mondo,
che per esser maggior più feccia mena,
bisogna spesso risciacquare il fondo;
e la natura, che si sente piena,
piglia una medicina di moría (LII)

(. . . this bulging belly of the world,
which being larger produces more dregs,
often needs to be thoroughly rinsed out;
and nature, which feels full,
takes a dose of pestilence as medicine).

---

[14] Cap. XXXI in F. Berni, *Opere* (Milan: Daelli, 1864). For the following
quotes refer back to the Chiòrboli ed. [tr.]

But nature has also "a great deal of the clown." Berni well perceives all its bitter contrasts and harsh dissonances, and he knows how to laugh at them while giving them artistic expression. In a letter in verse to Sebastiano del Piombo the painter, speaking of Michelangelo, their common friend, he writes:

Ad ogni modo è disonesto a dire
che voi, che fate e' legni e' sassi vivi,
abbiate poi com'asini a morire.
Basta che vivon le querci e gli olivi,
e' sorbi le cornacchie e' cervi e' cani,
e mille animalacci piú cattivi.
Ma questi son ragionamenti vani;
però lasciànli andar, ché non si dica
che noi siam mamalucchi o luterani. (LXIII)

(Anyway, it is dishonest to say
that you who make wood and stone come to life
have then to die like donkeys;
as long as oak and olive trees,
sorb-trees, crows, deer, dogs,
and thousands of worse animals, are living.
But these are vain reasonings,
let's forget all that, and just let it not be said
that we are mamelukes or lutherans.)

Chapter V.   COMIC IRONY IN CHIVALRESQUE POETRY

When Brunetière attacked modern scholarship and French literature of the Middle Ages, many critics—especially Romance specialists, and even including some from outside France—rose up in wild indignation to defend both fields.[1] Of course, the defense of contemporary erudition would have been more effective had its apologists not spitefully indulged in all sorts of vulgar insults against esthetic criticism while at the same time trying enthusiastically to defend the beautiful qualities of French epic and chivalresque poetry of the Middle Ages.

I recall, among others, Nyrop's defense on account of the ingenuous speciousness of his arguments.[2] "The poems have been criticized on the grounds that they are harsh and coarse and that the characters who act in them cannot lay claim to the title of heroes because all their efforts are directed toward nothing except *killing*." But how did he defend the poems from these charges of coarseness and cruelty? Well, he did not. "One may willingly concede," he wrote, "that many poets have sung and celebrated actions which, seen from the point of view of our time, can only be called cruelties, abominable and bestial cruelties; and that the heroes often vent their anger inhumanely on those who had the misfortune to fall in their power." At this point Nyrop gave a few examples and then, by way of apology, added that "the Middle Ages, when observed from today's point of view, was not at all different. Certainly, the early French poems cannot be blamed for any exaggeration, since history has preserved the memory of many similar cruelties."

[1] Ferdinand Brunetière, "L'érudition contemporaine et la littérature française du moyen âge," *Revue des Deux Mondes,* Vol. 49 (1879), 620–649, reprinted also in his *Etudes critiques sur l'histoire de la littérature française* (Paris, 1880).

[2] K. Nyrop, "Valore dell'Epopea," Bk. III, Chap. III of his *Storia dell'Epopea francese nel Medio Evo,* tr. [from Swedish] by E. Gorra (Florence, 1886), pp. 323–332.

Historical fidelity is a fine excuse with which to counter esthetic judgment! But even the most atrocious cruelties, like everything else, can be the subject matter of art: Achilles was extremely merciless when he dragged Hector's body around the walls of Troy. What was needed was to show that cruelty, in the French poems, was treated not only with historical faithfulness, which would have really mattered little, but also artistically, and this Nyrop could not do because, as he himself recognized,

from a psychological point of view the heroes are not very complex; their emotions, their moments of vacillation, and their inner turmoil are elements about which the poets almost never speak . . . Detailed psychological analyses are possible and may be of interest only in more advanced periods of civilization. The medieval poet is not familiar with these delicate shades of feeling; he recognizes only the most striking external signs; as far as he is concerned, men are either courageous or cowardly, happy or troubled, believers or heretics: whatever they are, they are thoroughly so, and the poet never wastes many words to communicate this to his listening or reading public.

Then, examining all the poems one by one, Nyrop was forced to recognize that religion, which, together with enthusiasm for war, was one of the main motives of the French epic, is a "puerile" conception; what's more, he said:

Religiosity recurs most of the time in the poems as something external, as something added on to the heroes, and therefore it is generally at odds with their actions. In other words: the heroes do not seem to be entirely convinced of the truth of all the beautiful Christian sayings that they are made to say; their character and their inner world are not in harmony with the meek and humane Christian dogmas. For this reason, there frequently emerges an insoluble contradiction which is markedly evident in their speech and actions. So, for instance, it is not uncommoñ for any one hero to forget himself in his prayers to such an extent as to add the worst threats if God should not grant his request. And I believe that Gautier and D'Avril are far off the mark when they contend that religiosity is the most important element of the epic.

Gautier's enthusiasm every time the heroes invoke God's name is sometimes ridiculous. Even the most common and trivial phrases in which angels are mentioned prompt his blissful and enraptured remarks: "Sublime, incomparable." And when he comes upon such a stereotyped line as "Foi que doi Dieu, le fils sainte Marie" ("the faith that God gives, the son of Holy Mary"), he calls it a forceful affirmation of faith. Taken as a whole, his point of view is so limited and so extremely Catholic that it is not worth the trouble to oppose. I conceive the religiosity of the heroes only as something which was in a sense added later, perhaps during the time of the Crusades, and for that reason it becomes only a concomitant but subordinated factor. Indeed, my opinion can also be supported by the fact that the clergy, especially the monks, are seldom placed in a light that is very favorable to them. If they want to aspire to the poets' favor, they must, like Turpin, present themselves with a sword at their side.[3]

I wanted to recall this because it seems to me that Nyrop's statement has too often been forgotten by those who, speaking with little knowledge about French epic, observe its serious and profound religious feelings and who knows how many other spirited and noble ideas, only then to say that such feelings and ideals could not find an echo in the Italian chivalric poets who flourished in a time of "skeptical indifference" and "pagan serenity," a time "devoid of aspirations," etc.

All these ready-made phrases are irrelevant and the explanation for the laughter of the Italian chivalresque poets must be sought elsewhere.

Irony of the subject matter and satire of the chivalresque life can already be found in medieval France and even in epic poems such as, for instance, *Aiol.* The mockery of the Emperor and the signs of his gradual degradation are already present in an early poem like *Ogier le Danois,* in which Charles no longer possesses his level-headed prudence, lets himself be easily overcome with anger, commits outrages and then is afraid of the vengeance of his victims. We see him gradually become an imbecile, the target of jokes, and morally corrupt. In *Garin de Montglane,* as is well known, he goes so far as to put up France as stake at the chessboard.

We can easily discover the reason for this degradation and mockery; it is to be found especially in those poems motivated by a desire to glorify some provincial hero, poems composed by trouvères in the service of vassals who, though not altogether rebellious, were almost completely independent and enjoyed laughing at the expense of imperial authority. Likewise, the mockery of

---

[3] The knights also allowed themselves to mock the rituals and ceremonies of chivalry, and this is something which happens in the very poems on the Crusades. In the *Antioche,* for example, there is a typical and delightful scene when the French knights leave the city on their way to fight against Kerboga. Their leader is Enguerrant de Saint-Pol, whose brightly polished helmet and armor shine resplendently in the sunlight. Once outside the city, the crusaders come to a stop. When an archbishop prays for heaven's blessing on them and wants to sprinkle them with holy water, Enguerrant objects and asks him not to stain his helmet: "Anqui le vourrai bel a Sarrasins mostrer" ("Ere long I like to show it gleaming to the Saracens"). For the text, see Pigeonneau, *Cycle de la Croisade,* pp. 90–91.

the life of chivalry and the degradation of the knights, who earlier had been exalted at the expense of the *vilan,* will be found in the poems that were no longer sung at court or in the castles. If our good Tassoni could have read in the *Siège de Neuville* the feat of those clever Flemish weavers headed by Simone Banin, perhaps he would not have boasted of being the creator of the mock-heroic poem. Even this is to be found in France, in its purest state.

What then? Rajna observes that "the dissemination of these poems southward over the Alps seems to have occurred very early and later to have slackened; otherwise, it would be difficult to ex-plain how Italy had known the archaic forms of the *chansons de geste* better than the later forms—to the extent that it retained both the narratives or narrative forms that would later change or be forgotten in France—while it remained almost completely un-aware of the hybrid creations which introduced into the genre the element of the marvelous from the novels of adventure."[4] Rajna goes on to outline the most common type of chivalric poem preva-lent in the Franco-Italian period, the type to which Pulci's *Mor-gante* very largely belongs. But it should also be noted—in Rajna's own words—that "the Tuscan literature of adventure, whether in prose or verse, is directly linked to the preceding periods . . . There is no lack of prose texts that were made from rhymed versions or from a combination of these and the earlier French or Franco-Italian forms."[5]

The fact is that when in France the earliest poems were rendered into novels and reached the people, the epic was dead; in Italy, instead, it was not the epic—for this was not possible— but chivalric poetry that began to emerge when prose or rhymed versions of the French, Franco-Italian or Venetian poems were in-troduced in Tuscany, where they found their appropriate meter, the octave. And in all this movement the subject matter of the epic either remained as it was—that is, degraded—or, while seek-ing to become more refined, it became contaminated (in the classical sense of the word) and also elevated itself enough to achieve serious dramatization.

What, therefore, do the skepticism of the times, the indifference, the lack of all ideals have to do with this if, on the contrary, the

---

[4] Pio Rajna, *Le fonti dell'Orlando furioso,* 2nd ed. (Florence, Sansoni, 1900), p. 14. [tr.]

[5] *Ibid.,* p. 17. [tr.]

Italian chivalresque poets are inclined gradually to uplift and
ennoble this material, to long for, and almost to evoke as in a
dream, those ideals by cleansing the heroes of excessive blood and
by rendering them more gentle and human? And if the Italian
poets still find it difficult to take those heroes seriously, it is not because they see them devoid of those ideals and no longer inspired
by the old religious feelings, but because it was practically impossible that anyone should take them seriously, after the harsh-
ness and coarseness with which they were characterized (with only
rare exceptions) in medieval poetry. It was unavoidable that
those heroes, all monolithic, all made of the same mold, should
appear as puppets to the cultivated and mature poets who read
and admired the classics.

Yet the common people and also the noblemen still enjoyed
hearing about their improbable deeds. With the common people,
this is understandable: in Naples, in Palermo, they enjoy them
intensely to this day. The material changes and grows; it draws its
sustenance and character from the emotions, customs and aspirations of the people to whom it is presented, acquiring a rough style
of which the people are easily satisfied. The people believe;
especially the southern people—rustic, passionate, and still almost
primitive—preserve to this day all those elements of innocent
wonder and superstitious and fanatical credulity which make possible the rise and growth of legends. And if Garibaldi, dressed in
flaming red, should pass in the midst of these people, he would
immediately and spontaneously be invested with the oldest
legendary attributes: he would be believed invulnerable, and
his sword would have a hair from the head of Saint Rosalia, the
patroness of Palermo, just as Roland's Durendal had a strand of
the Virgin's hair. After all, isn't it true that, although we lack the
blissful ignorance of the people, we all have a legendary and epic
vision of Garibaldi, the man whose life was, and was intended to
be, a true creation in everything, even in the manner of dress,
above and beyond any notion of all contingent reality; and isn't it
true that our epic view of Garibaldi would be offended even by
the slightest attempt to expose some discordant trait or by any
historical document bent on diminishing him in some aspect? And
yet we could no longer be satisfied today with a true and authentic
Garibaldian epic, that is, one that has emerged from the people
and is endowed with those ingenuous and primitive legendary
characteristics; just as, on the other hand, we are not satisfied with

the lyrico-epic compositions on this hero, compositions in which the poet tries to replace the collective imagination with his own individual fantasy, but is unsuccessful because it was the hero himself who created his own life with his own will and feelings, a life of epic dimensions, so that his history is in itself epic and the poet's imagination could add nothing to it, just as the ingenuous and marvelous exaggerations created by the collective imagination of the people would lessen it and make it appear ridiculous. To try to give it poetic representation would make it a parody of the epic, like, for instance, Cesare Pascarella's *La scoperta dell'America*.

For the common people, history is never written, or if it is, they ignore it or are indifferent to it. They create their own history and in a way that responds to their emotions and hopes. Within the range of chivalric poetry, the common people might have believed, at best, in one story: the famous *Cronaca* by pseudo-Turpin. For, whenever the need arose, this book could verify, to cite one instance, that the giant by the name of Ferraú or Ferracutus "belonged to the species of Goliath," whose height was "quasi cubitis XX, facies erat longa quasi unius cubiti et nasus illius unius palmi mensurati et brachia et crura ejus quatuor cubitum erant et digiti ejus tribus palmis" ("almost 20 cubits tall and his face was almost 20 inches long and his nose measured one full span and his arms were four cubits and the fingers were three span in length"). But this was totally unnecessary, for the people are always motivated by a different type of need: the need to believe and not to doubt in the least what they like to believe. The doubt could arise in the late pseudo-literary renovators of the French epic when, having transformed in their own way the old legends, they would bring up Turpin's or Saint Dionysius' chronicles:

Et qui ice voudrai a mançogne tenir
se voist lire l'estoire en France, a Paris.

(And if anyone holds this to be a lie
let him go to Paris, France, to read the history.)

From this one can see that not even in this respect would our chivalresque poets have been original whenever, by way of apology, they would add: *Turpin lo dice* ("According to Turpin").

*

What happens when this chivalresque poetry rises—either out of whim or curiosity or because of the charm and beauty it may have

—from the public squares where it had fallen and returns to the palaces and royal courts? But first of all we have to bear in mind the nature, tastes, and customs of these courts, to which it ascends! We all know what Lorenzo de' Medici's court was like and what were his habits, amusements, and intellectual scope; and this would be enough—even if we did not stress as much as we should the different personalities and education of the various poets—to explain to a large extent why Pulci's *Morgante* differs so much from both Boiardo's *Orlando innamorato* and Ariosto's *Furioso*. The *Morgante* is in perfect keeping with the court of Lorenzo, who enjoys using the popular speech and who writes for the common people with intent to parody, as in his *Nencia da Barberino*. Lorenzo has a special taste for parody, and this is evident also from his *Beoni,* which is a parody of Dante, a literary parody, whereas the *Nencia* is a parody of the popular expression. In his preface to Lorenzo's poetry, Carducci remarked:

It is indeed true that Lorenzo was more ready and eager to travesty and parody the peasants' emotions and speech than to portray them; for his *Rispetti,* reprinted several times in recent years, show clearly that the Tuscan folk had more gentle feeling, refinement of imagination, and elegance of speech than Lorenzo de' Medici, called the Magnificent, and his courtier Luigi Pulci cared to recognize in them. The latter, as is wont of courtly writers, wanted to show how much he valued his protector as a powerful poet by imitating him in his *Beca da Dicomano.* And, as is typical of imitators, while attempting to outdo him, he only exaggerated him and produced a flaunting display of the strange and grotesque where Lorenzo, even while writing parody, had kept close to a tastefully restrained tone.[6]

But it is clear that the parodic intention inevitably infuses caricature into the form, since he who wants to imitate someone else must necessarily capture his most conspicuous traits and insist on them; and such insistence inevitably produces caricature. The presence of that pious woman, Lucrezia Tornabuoni, could also explain to us, at least to some extent, the religious disguise that Pulci chose to give his poem, which, in my view, is also a parody like everything else.

All one needs to do, to produce a sense of irreverence, is to treat religion with the buffoonish language of the populace. I shall recall, in this regard, the answer that Belli sent to Luigi L. Bonaparte's suggestion that he undertake a translation of the book of St.

6 Giosuè Carducci, Preface to Lorenzo de' Medici, *Poesie* (Florence: Barbèra, 1859); see also his *Primi saggi,* vol. II of *Opere* (Bologna, 1889), p. 39.

Matthew into Roman dialect. But this irreverence which stems from the buffoonish language of the people does not in itself indicate an anti-religious attitude. And let me also recall an anecdote circulating in Sicily about another great poet in dialect, Domenico Tempio, who is well known on the island and yet totally unknown to the Continent. Summoned one day by the Bishop of Catania and paternally urged to stop singing obscene songs and to write instead a holy song on Christ's passion and death so as to set a good example for the people during Holy Week, Tempio replied that he would gladly do it since he was a very faithful and devout believer; indeed, he decided to give the bishop a taste of it right away, improvising on the spot a couple of lines against Pontius Pilate that were so obscene that they promptly dissipated Monsignor's intention of offering to the people of Catania a good example of contrition during Holy Week.

All the controversies which have arisen around Pulci's irreverence toward religion, or rather around his impiety and atheism, can appear in truth only to be futile, when one fully understands the spirit of the poem and the quality and motivation of its irony and laughter.

It is not possible, or it is extremely unfair, to judge the *Morgante maggiore* in and by itself, as De Sanctis, for example, did at one time, when he believed and tried to show that Pulci, upon writing his poem, was not truly and profoundly aware of his purpose; for this reason the critic condemned as defects in the poet the childish situations, the rudimental psychology of the characters, the repetitions in the plot, etc.[7] Pulci, on the contrary, is fully conscious of his aim; and between the two types projected by De Sanctis—i.e., those who say foolish things with comic intention and provoke laughter not at themselves but at what they say, as opposed to those who say foolish things out of sheer foolishness and make others laugh at themselves and not at what they say—the author of *Morgante* belongs undoubtedly to the first type and not to the second. Pulci says foolish things with comic or, to be more exact, parodic intention, and he makes the reader laugh,

---

[7] Francesco De Sanctis, *Scritti varii inediti o rari* (Naples: Morano, 1898), vol. I, 248 ff. Later, in his *Storia della letteratura italiana,* De Sanctis corrected this view of Pulci and of his poem. I have cited his earlier statement only because we can profit from this eminent critic's error (which, after all, was rectified) by placing in the proper light, through this easy refutation of mine, which of the two comic types that he mentions is the truly valid one with respect to Pulci.

although, as we shall see later, not as much as Attilio Momigliano would have us believe in a recent book of his.[8]

Earlier I mentioned Cesare Pascarella's *La scoperta dell'America*. From an esthetic viewpoint, one can say that Pulci's position with respect to chivalresque material is somewhat similar to Pascarella's position with respect to the idea of a commoner narrating the discovery of America. In fact, the Roman poet, while in a tavern, unexpectedly comes upon (or pretends to come upon) a wise man of the people who is relating that discovery to his friends and who is moved by Columbus' glory and hardships. Who would think of attributing to the author the nonsense of the man's tale? Or the ridiculous childishness of those dialogues with the Portuguese king of Spain? Or all the other marvels—no less ridiculous and infantile—of the voyage, the arrival, and the return? And it should be noted that, at a certain point, all these marvels also produce some reaction of disbelief in the audience: "But you, how do you know all these things?" they ask, and the narrator: "Ah! There is the history book" (i.e., 'According to Turpin'). Scattered here and there are comparisons which are seemingly intended to prove something with utmost evidence but turn out to prove nothing; and certain heated tirades of scorn or admiration; and certain explanations in which the commoner's rudimentary logic delights in its attempts at explaining and justifying some extraordinary event or incident; and certain moments of transport which are funny not because the narrator intended them to be funny but rather because of the false deductions, unsuited and jarring images, or incongruous expressions.

Ciaripensa, e te scopre er cannocchiale.

(He thinks it over, and discovers the telescope.)

Who would dream of saying that Pascarella's intention here is to ridicule Galileo? But even though he treats this tavern tale with complete objectivity, the author cannot help but laugh, within himself, at this commoner who speaks in such a way of the glory of Columbus and other great Italians and of the discovery of America. And this secret laughter of his imparts almost an air of gaiety, an atmosphere of irresistible mirth around that objective presentation. The comical intention behind this objective presen-

[8] *L'indole e il riso di Luigi Pulci* (Rocca San Casciano: Cappelli, 1907), cited earlier.

tation of the commoner's nonsense never comes into the open; the poet never shows a glimpse of himself.

Now truly this cannot be said of Pulci. While Pascarella simply depicts reality, Pulci often mimics it for parody's sake. But we must not ascribe to him all the nonsensical, vulgar and childish expressions of the wandering minstrels or of the romances and epics from France or northern Italy, for, on the contrary, he manifestly mocks that literature through mimicry and parody. That would be like taking seriously something that was done in jest; or it would be like accusing Pascarella of having derided Columbus' glorious achievement by retelling the commoner's story. Pulci himself is in no way thinking of ridiculing chivalry and religion. He has a good time parodying the village troubadours and singing the epic and chivalresque material in their manner and with their language, their infantile psychology and stereotyped methods of creativity. From time to time he follows and interprets popular emotion in some moving scene or in some action which arouses anger or pity or indignation, etc. Naturally, if on one hand all this represents for Pulci a pastime and a game, on the other hand, simply because he dedicates to it his art, his work and time, it cannot but be taken seriously as well. Thus it is not infrequently that he really identifies with the narrative, though always through the emotions, the logic and psychology of the common people, and creates expressions of great effectiveness. It is true that then, quite suddenly, he breaks the serious spell with a roar of laughter; but, in my view, this never has a satiric motivation, for such outbursts are often in a burlesque and popular vein and also here the poet is often following and interpreting the feelings of the people.

Therefore I think that Momigliano is wrong and also contradicts himself when he states that "the laughter in the *Morgante* is subjective in the sense that Pulci's temperament spontaneously and unrestrainably bursts into the epic material." Indeed Momigliano adds: "In this sense, the *Morgante* is one of the most subjective epic poems that I know of and could be described as 'the world of chivalry viewed through a jovial temperament.' What's more, after so much controversy as to whether Morgante or Gano is the protagonist, I believe that the only character who dominates all action and around whom all action turns is the author himself; aside from him, the poem has no protagonist."[9] A

9 *Ibid.*, pp. 120–121.

few pages before, Momigliano had stated that "in a period when laughter was more carefree than satiric, the laughter of *Morgante* is only a veneer of the time which, overlaid on the traditional material, produces a deformation merely of its surface." And earlier, in his inquiry into and study of Pulci's temperament in the first part of the volume, Momigliano had remarked:

> Indeed, while the man cried, the poet laughed. To endure writing a jocose poem like *Morgante* took no small amount of inner strength at a time when his heart was torn by ever recurring misfortunes and his life threatened by hunger or imprisonment for debts. The case of poets who laugh at their own travails is not uncommon, but it is indeed extremely rare to find the example of an unfortunate poet who involves his artistic activity in a work where laughter is never clouded by tears. It is a miracle which, to some extent, was probably due to the influence of the Renaissance.[10]

Incidentally, I confess that I cannot see the spirit of Italian Renaissance as being so cheerful, as Momigliano and others see it. I am suspicious of the invitations to enjoy life, especially when they are so persistent and determined to appear carefree. I am suspicious of those who want to be happy at all costs. As for the *Trionfo di Bacco e d'Arianna,* it is only the Horatian *carpe diem*:

> Tu ne quaesieris, scire nefas, quem mihi, quem tibi
> finem di dederint. . . .

> (Do not inquire—we cannot be allowed to find out
> what end the Gods set for me, what for you. . . .)

Can we really call cheerful somebody who stuns himself in order not to think? If anything, it could be the philosophy of wise men but not the merriment of young people. And how many sad things do those famous carnival songs say to those who know how to read into them!

But let's drop this topic, for it would be idle to talk about it now, especially as I think that Pulci depicts everything from the characteristic perspective of the Florentine temperament and his language is the clownish language of the people, and what he intends to mimic and parody in his *Morgante* is the ideas and emotions that the people have with respect to the epic and chivalresque material as expressed by the minstrels. And I repeat that, in my view, the *Morgante* is not that monument of mirth that Momigliano would have us believe it is.

[10] *Ibid.,* p. 113.

To explain what Momigliano regards as a "miracle," it is enough to direct our attention to what I have just said, and to mind not so much the poet's temperament but his objective. If the poet's life is wretched, and if in writing "Io vo' dire una frottola" he confesses: "I hurt when I laugh," and "I shall never be happy," and "I never liked myself and I still don't"; if he felt inclined toward sadness and melancholy from the time he was born, as Momigliano himself shows by quoting from other works besides this *frottola,* which was written in the later years of his life; if Pulci "had two ways of mitigating his pain, either to resign himself, a remedy he rarely resorted to, or *to laugh at it in the manner of the humorists,* truly a consolation for people in despair"; and if "this sad humor, which is subjective in Pulci and not objective, is lacking almost completely in the *Morgante*";[11] if all this is true, how is it that, contrary to his sad humor, Pulci's laughter becomes objective in a "natural, unrestrainable eruption of his temperament into the epic material"? How can Pulci be the real protagonist of his poem?

If only he had been! But if in his letters and in the *frottola* Pulci can sometimes laugh at his afflictions in the style of the humorists, he never succeeds in objectifying his natural humoristic disposition in the poem. He lives two lives, but cannot make them live in his poem. "A painful duality," exclaims at this point Momigliano, "which dooms him to play the part of a happy mask, but when his imagination cools down—and it is from his imagination that the easy verses flowed like an inexhaustibly jubilant group of characters from the doors of an enchanted palace—the grief of his everyday life of torment, by contrast, makes him feel his anguish more sharply than ever."[12] But then, if it is a mask, it cannot be his temperament that naturally and unrestrainably erupts into the epic material!

But it isn't even a mask. There is practically nothing in the poem that is truly subjective: the *Morgante* is "chivalresque material infused with a plebeian soul," as stated by Cesareo, who sees in the giant armed with a clapper and in Margutte the people themselves as they look at their own image in the mirror of their coarse and sincere naturalism. The giant is "ignorant, voracious, aggressive and violent; he is a mocker, but he has no perfidy and is ready to carry out the most arduous deeds at a single sign from

11 *Ibid.,* p. 70. [tr.]
12 *Ibid.,* p. 88. [tr.]

his master. He represents the unaware and sudden force of the people which is aptly directed by a feeling capable of developing their hidden qualities: honesty, justice, indulgence, devotion, and affection. Margutte, on the other hand, represents the unbelieving and unfeeling people, the abject, shameless, mocking, devious, criminal, and arrogant villain." Therefore the poem's true protagonist is Morgante, the good common people who are swept up by the extravagant adventures of the French paladins and who participate in these adventures in their own way. Pulci has intended nothing else in his parody.

I cannot pause now to point out all the false consequences that Momigliano draws from what I consider his erroneous conviction that laughter in the *Morgante* is subjective. He is in good company. Rajna too thinks that the. *Morgante* is new and original "in those episodes where the author introduces curious characters of his own making and gives full vent to his imagination and reason, *especially where he shows his own self* and in the attitude he adopts toward his own work."[13] Now, with respect to his true self, if we are to stop at Momigliano's inquiry, Pulci never reveals it at all in his poem. Why, he plays instead the part of a happy mask! It seems to me a serious error to attribute directly to the poet what should be attributed to the feeling, logic, psychology, and buffoonish language of the common people in the parody which he makes of them.

For example, Momigliano observes at one point: "I would not, however, venture to sustain the perfect innocence of Pulci when Ulivieri appears to explain the mystery of the Trinity with that example of the candle, which doesn't explain anything."[14] As though all popular literature were not filled with these explanations which explain nothing! And furthermore, if the comparison already is found in the *Orlando,* what does Pulci's cunning have to do with it? Later, while treating Fuligatto's conversion, Momigliano remarks: "It is however a fact that those conversions and baptisms—considering the speed and frequency with which they were performed and the excessive fervor of the neophytes—do tend to make us somewhat suspicious."[15] But this is one of the typical features of the French epic, and one that shows in fact how childish was its religious conception. As soon as a city was con-

---

[13] Rajna, p. 20.
[14] Momigliano, pp. 140–41. [tr]
[15] *Ibid.*, p. 140. [tr.]

quered, the victors required the infidels to convert; those who refused faced the edge of the sword, while the baptized turned at once into most zealous Christians. What does Pulci have to do with this? With respect to the episode in canto XXI where Orlando is ridiculed by some young rascals while he is crossing a town on his Vegliantino which is so battered that it can hardly stand, Momigliano says that Pulci has no feeling for chivalresque majesty. He then adds:

For our poet, laughter is one of the great laws, and to it everyone must pay tribute. Pulci thus outlines both the serious and the ridiculous traits in his characters and from time to time he reduces them to human size. In the episode just mentioned it may seem that he is trying to poke fun at Orlando, but it is not so. An unvanquished champion who rides a feeble palfrey—here Vegliantino also is reduced from the traditional dignity of the heroes' mounts—is he not a champion who has been subjected to a *deminutio capitis*? Does he not resemble slightly the Knight of the Mournful Countenance? Isn't it possible for such a thing to happen to a paladin? But just let someone brazenly step forward and try to mock him, and you will see that he is not a Don Quijote but an authentic champion. And this is the way in which Orlando, after being momentarily degraded, quickly rises again. *The source has something much like this (Orlando, L, 30–37).* We are already close to mockery, but have as yet fully to reach it. Mockery will only appear when laughter will burst out as a deliberate rebellion of reason.[16]

Once again things are attributed to Pulci which, first of all, are found in his source as well as in other later poems such as *Aiol* and *Florent et Octavien*. Thus, that certain particular tendency to be emotional which Momigliano considers unnatural in warriors of the stamina of the paladins, is already found, as is well known, in the French epic where there are countless lines and stereotyped epic formulas about faintings and swoonings of warriors and knights and sometimes even of entire armies: "Trois fois se pasme sor le corant destrier," "Cent milie franc s'en pasment cuntre terre" ("Three times he faints on the running horse," "100,000 Franks faint and fall to the ground").

Given Momigliano's conception of humor as "laughter which penetrates more subtly and deeply into its own object," and as "evidence, also when it does not rise to the contemplation of a general fact, of a mind accustomed to seek the essence of things," one can understand how he, with a great deal of good will, can find humor also in *Morgante,* in spite of the fact that he himself

---

[16] *Ibid.,* p. 250. [tr.]

had said before that "the kind of laughter in the poem does not stem from a profound psychology"; that "this is caused by Pulci's ineptitude as well as by the material itself, which is usually satisfied with inconsistent characters";[17] that Pulci "sees especially the ridiculous of the physical, the ridiculous of the forms, postures, and movements of a body"; and that his laughter is usually superficial and "in its almost constant levity it portrays the spirit and literature of the times."[18] But now Momigliano thinks that "grief, tolerance, sympathy, etc. are all accessory elements" of humor, which in conclusion is, as stated by Masci, "the general sense of the comic"[19] and nothing more.

Taken in this general sense, humor can be found anywhere. It can be found in Ulivieri's statement after his horse has thrown him before the very eyes of Meridiana:

Alla mia vita non caddi ancor mai,
ma ogni cosa vuol cominciamento (*Morgante,* VII, 68)

(In my whole life I never fell once,
but there must be a first time to everything);

and in Meridiana's answer:

Usanza è in guerra cader dal destriere,
ma chi si fugge non suol mai cadere.

(It is customary in war to fall from a horse,
but he who flees is not wont to fall.)

Humor! Rinaldo, forgetting Luciana, falls in love with Antea and entrusts Luciana to Ulivieri, appealing to him to serve her with all care; to which Ulivieri replies:

. . . Cosí va la fortuna;
cércati d'altro amante, Lucïana.
Da me sarai d'ogni cosa servito. (XVI, 23)

(So goes luck;
find yourself another lover, Luciana.
I shall serve you in everything.)

Momigliano calls this reply "concise, philosophical, humorous," and so on.[20]

But it is decidedly not so. True humor cannot be found in the

---

[17] *Ibid.,* p. 154. [tr.]
[18] *Ibid.,* pp. 119–20. [tr.]
[19] *Ibid.,* p. 154. [tr.]
[20] *Ibid.,* p. 157. [tr.]

Morgante. It might have been found there, if Pulci had been able to infuse his own sorrows and miseries into some of his characters or into some episodes of the poem, and if he had laughed at his own sorrows as he does in his *frottola* and in some of his letters. It might have been found if his irony—the vain appearance of that foolish, puerile, or grotesque chivalresque world—had at some point been able to achieve comic dramatization through the poet's emotion. Actually Pulci not only cannot and does not see himself in the drama, but he cannot even see the drama in the object of the artistic representation. How, then, can one speak of humor? I mean true humor, which is not at all what Momigliano, following Masci, believes it to be. As for the other kind of humor—the humor understood in the broader and more usual sense which we have already discussed—of that kind, indeed, Pulci has as much as can be found in the combined work of a hundred of those English writers who would be considered as true humorists by Nencioni and Arcoleo. This is unquestionable.

*

I dwelt upon the *Morgante* because, of the three Italian chivalresque poems, it is the one endowed with a greater and more far-reaching irony: an irony which, according to Schlegel's definition, reduces the literary material to a perpetual parody and consists in the writer's not losing, not even in the moments of pathos, his awareness of the unreality of his own creation.

In the two other poets, Boiardo and Ariosto, the artistic purpose is more serious. It is necessary, however, to delve deeply into this greater seriousness. Pulci is a *popular* poet in the sense that he does not lift the material at all from the level of the people but rather keeps it there and makes a parody of it in a bourgeois court like that of Lorenzo who, as I have said, had a taste for parody. Boiardo is a *courtly* poet in the sense that he has, to use Rajna's words, "a profoundly sympathetic liking for the chivalric customs and feelings: love, kindness, courage, and courtesy"; and if "he is neither reluctant to jest with the subject nor remorseful for exposing his characters to mockery, it is because his aim is to honor bravery, courtesy, and love, rather than Orlando and Ferraguto."[21] Boiardo then is a courtly poet in the sense that he writes in order to provide diversion and welcomed recreation to a

[21] Rajna, p. 29. [tr.]

court which—living in comfortable and elegant leisure, and passionately taken by the vicissitudes of Guinevere and Iseult and by the adventures of the knights-errant—would have been incapable of accepting the French paladins, had they been presented as devoid of love and courtesy. As for Ariosto, one must take into account the circumstances of his life and his relationship with the house of Este; from this point of view and in another sense, he too is a courtly poet; but when it comes to the material itself that he treats in his work, then Ariosto is concerned only with the serious norms of art.

We have already seen that even in France the world of epic and chivalresque poetry had lost all seriousness years before. How could the Italian poets treat seriously something that had ceased to be serious a long time before? Comic irony was inevitable. And yet, as De Sanctis aptly remarks, "the writer who creates a comic work is not exempt from the serious norms of art."[22] Now, among the three poets mentioned, Ariosto has the greatest respect for the norms of art; Pulci has the least respect, not because he is not an artist, as De Sanctis thought at first, but rather because of what I have already mentioned, namely the purpose that motivates the poet's work.

Parody and caricature are unquestionably motivated by the writer's satiric or simply burlesque intention. Satire and mockery consist in a ridiculous alteration of the model; consequently they are measurable only if related to the qualities of the model and particularly to those qualities which are most markedly conspicuous and which represent an exaggeration already in the model itself. The writer of a parody or caricature will insist on these markedly noticeable features; he will highlight them, and exaggerate what is already exaggerated. In order to achieve this, the artist is inevitably bound to strain his expressive means and alter his sketch, his voice or, at any rate, his expression, in a strange, clumsy and even grotesque fashion. In short, parody requires that violence be done to art and to its serious norms. When working with a blemish or defect of art or nature, exaggeration is the only means to achieve laughter. The end result of this exaggeration must necessarily be something monstrous, something that, considered in and by itself, is devoid of truth and consequently of beauty; to understand its truth and therefore its beauty, it is neces-

22 De Sanctis, p. 286. [tr.]

sary to examine the end result of a parody by relating it to the original model. Thus, we leave the sphere of pure fantasy. In order to laugh at or ridicule the blemish or defect, we must also jest with the tools of art; we must be conscious of our game, which may be cruel, or may not have any malicious intentions, or may even have serious intentions as in the case of Aristophanes and his caricatures.

Let me repeat therefore that if Pulci fails to respect the serious norms of art in his comic poem, it is not because he is lacking as an artist. The same cannot be said of Boiardo, who is more serious not in artistic purpose, which he lacks, but rather in his objective of pleasing his court while pursuing at the same time his inclination and enjoyment. It has even been said that Boiardo treats chivalry seriously in his poem. Rajna—who, as is well known, in his book on the sources of Ariosto's *Orlando furioso,* seems to have set about to exalt Boiardo at the expense of "his continuator"— has posed this question with respect to the distinction to be drawn between the *Innamorato* and the *Furioso:*

Shall we base this distinction on what is known as "Ariosto's irony"? It has been suggested that Ariosto, with a skeptical smile, dissolved Boiardo's edifice into a cloud of smoke and turned the characters of the *Innamorato* into phantoms. This would be fine if it were true. The problem is that the edifice and characters were already a phantasmagoria for the Count of Scandiano. If Ariosto does not believe in the world he sings, his predecessor and master is even more of an unbeliever; if Ariosto makes fun of that world, Boiardo on occasion makes no less sport of it; if there is irony in the *Furioso,* there is no lack of it in the *Innamorato* either.[23]

And a few pages before:

To hear somebody talk about the *Innamorato* in terms of burlèsque and humor must certainly be cause for considerable astonishment. We are so used to hearing, in a variety of tones and by men who are very authoritative and judicious, that Boiardo sings the wars of Albracca and the adventures of Orlando and Rinaldo with the same seriousness and conviction with which Tasso a century later was to extol the Christian ventures in Palestine and the conquest of Jerusalem. This is an error, which I think unnecessary to refute . . . It does not take long to perceive that there is a real conflict between Boiardo and his artistic world, a conflict that differs only in intensity and tone from the one that prevented Pulci from identifying with his material. For, to all cultured Italians of the fifteenth century, all those terrible thrusts and slashes, which by comparison would have dwarfed Homer's heroes, were quite ridiculous; and ridiculous appeared that chopping and mincing of flesh

23 Rajna, pp. 34–35. [tr.]

and armor on the most worthless pretexts, or even for no reason at all; ridiculous were the profound meditations on love which absorbed the soul completely for hours on end, and suppressed all trace of consciousness. In short, to the cultured contemporaries of Boiardo, all the exaggerations of the chivalric romances were ridiculous. How can one expect that a man saturated with classical culture and endowed with unshakeable good sense could contemplate this world and present it without ever breaking out in laughter? Boiardo does, in fact, laugh and does his best to make people laugh. Even in the midst of the most serious narratives he utters jokes and witticisms, and more than once he creates episodes which could be taken as invented by Cervantes in order to mock chivalry and its heroes.[24]

In this way Rajna thinks he is defending Boiardo from an injustice. His mistake, as pointed out by Cesareo after the new edition of Rajna's book,[25] was that he treated the question of the relation between Boiardo and Ariosto without preparing himself adequately to make esthetic judgments. And yet De Sanctis, in one of his Zurich lectures on chivalric poetry, had already expressed a splendid critical insight:

The poetic faculty *par excellence* is the creative fantasy. The poet, however, does not create only with the esthetic faculties, for all faculties work together. The poet is not only a poet: while his fantasy forms the image, his intellect and senses do not remain inoperative. A poet may have a great power of artistic creativity and be poor in imagination, commit errors in the design and make historical and geographical blunders: these defects do not affect the essence of poetry. But if a poet who has these faculties to a high degree, including a good design and a perfect technical execution, has a weak creative fantasy, he will be incapable of putting life into what he sees: the lack of the creative fantasy is death for a poet.

This is how the distinction should be made. Up to now we have no right to call Boiardo's poetic genius into question, for the defects that we have enumerated are dependent upon other faculties. In order to evaluate him as a poet, it is necessary first to see to what an extent he can create and give form to images.

He is very inventive and he is the Italian poet who has gathered the largest and most varied poetic material not only from the point of view of quantity but of quality as well. To be sure, inventiveness is a primary requisite in a poet, and in this respect Boiardo is superior to Pulci. But, far from being sufficient, inventiveness is the least essential element in art. Dumas leaves to his secretaries the task of collecting the materials and keeps for himself the task of infusing life into them. Once Boiardo

---

[24] *Ibid.*, pp. 27–28. [tr.]
[25] See G. A. Cesareo, "La fantasia dell'Ariosto," a study published first in *Nuova Antologia* and then in *Critica militante* (Messina: Trimarchi, 1907).

has gathered his material, does he know how to work with it successfully? This is the question. He does not leave it plain and bare as does Pulci; he has the faculty of conception and gives each event and character the necessary traits for them to acquire their own physiognomy. He is not satisfied with merely sketching a character; he is actually one of the outstanding painters of Italian literature. Few writers know how to draw a character with more assurance and competence.

What is there left for the poet to do? To show that his characters are alive. The one who gave them a certain form and certain characteristics must now give them life. The original *conception* must evolve into *situation*. Even the most emotional characters do not always behave emotionally. For the determining traits to become effectively realized, the artist must choose the right circumstances so that the inner forces of his characters may reveal themselves through them. A true esthetic situation exists when a character is placed in a set of circumstances that is most favorable for it to manifest itself. But Boiardo does not know how to turn the conception into situation.[26]

In his essay on Ariosto's poetic imagination, Cesareo, who elaborates and defines more precisely De Sanctis' splendid intuition, observes:

Whenever a created character is truly living in the poet's imagination, it will reveal itself completely no matter in what circumstances it may find itself. The poet does not have to select anything, because that creature is free, autonomous, independent of the poet himself; as such, it can only find itself in situations to which it is compelled by its character as opposed to the other characters around it. The situations assert themselves; they are not chosen by the poet, whose only job is to see to it that in every situation, even the least dramatic, the character appear whole and with all the traits of his personality. One situation only will therefore be sufficient for the character to express itself and we will know roughly what it will do in "more favorable" situations. The whole character of Farinata is already in the first lines with which he addresses Dante; Hamlet's character is already in the scene of his audience at court; Don Abbondio's is already in his walk towards the *bravi* at the beginning of the novel. Undoubtedly, each successive situation makes the character more intense and better defined, but any situation is an esthetic situation.[27]

In Cesareo's judgment, what Boiardo lacks is precisely a full vision of the character, and I agree with him. I am also at odds with another of De Sanctis' observations, namely that "Boiardo's pedantic aims lead him to treat seriously what is essentially comical."[28] Frankly, I cannot see any evidence of such didactic aims in Boiardo; neither can I see that his intention was to be

26 De Sanctis, pp. 304–05. [tr.]
27 Cesareo, pp. 41–42. [tr.]
28 De Sanctis, p. 298. [tr.]

serious and that he ended up being funny only "because of the compelling influence of his time." If, as De Sanctis himself points out, Boiardo "laughs at his own inventions," then he did not intend to be serious. As a matter of fact, my view is that Boiardo is to be blamed for the very reason that led Rajna to believe that he was defending him from unjust criticism: namely because—being a true nobleman and inspired by a profound feeling for chivalric customs, i.e., love, kindness, bravery, courtesy—*he did not intend to be serious,* as he could have in view of his natural feelings and as he should have out of respect for the serious norms of art. And his desire not to be serious did not produce true laughter as it should have, for only one kind of laughter is appropriate to such artistic material: the laughter that results at the level of form, and form is above all what is lacking in Boiardo. So that Rajna is right when he says, as quoted above, that "it doesn't take long to perceive that there is a real conflict between Boiardo and his artistic world, a conflict that differs only in intensity and tone from the one which prevented Pulci from identifying with his material." But Boiardo's inferiority with respect to Pulci and to Ariosto is precisely in the *intensity* and *tone* of his laughter. He cared only to amuse himself and others, and he failed to see that his intention to lift that material above the popular level and to reject the Pulcian manner of deliberate parody required that he should respect the serious norms of art, as Ariosto did.

It is definitely not true that the poet of the *Furioso,* with a skeptical smile, dissolves the edifice of the *Innamorato* into smoke and turns its characters into phantoms. On the contrary, he supplies both edifice and characters with the elements that were lacking: a consistency and a foundation of imaginative truth and esthetic coherence.

We need to come to a clear understanding on the question of the poet's not believing in the reality of his poetic world or in whatever world he portrays. But it might be said that no representation exists that can be believed as a reality, and this holds not only for the artist but for anyone else as well, no matter if created by art or if it be the representation we humans make of ourselves, of other people, and of life. The artistic image and the image that normally comes to us through our senses are, in essence, one and the same.

Nevertheless, we refer to the image obtained through our senses as *true,* and to the one created by art as *fictitious.* But to understand the difference between the two kinds of representation we

must talk in terms not of *reality* but rather of *will,* and only insofar as artistic fiction is *willed* (by willed I do not mean obtained
through an act of the will for purposes alien to artistic creation,
but rather willed and loved for its own sake, devoid of any other
motive), whereas the image of the senses does not depend on
whether we will it or not: it comes into being merely because we
are endowed with senses. Therefore the former is free, while the
latter is not. And while one is an image or form of sensations, the
other—artistic fiction—is a creation of form.

The artistic process actually begins only when a figuration develops a will of its own in our mind; that is to say, when it *wills
itself* in and by itself, and generates, by the mere fact that it wills
itself, a movement (a technique) capable of bringing it into realiza-
tion outside ourselves. If the figuration lacks this self-contained
will, which is the movement itself of the image, then it is no more
than a common psychic phenomenon—an image which is not
willed by itself, an automatic spiritual phenomenon—insofar as it
does not depend on our volition but comes into being in us as a
result of a sense perception.

We all have, to some extent, a will that generates those movements which enable us to create our own lives. This creation, which
everyone makes of his own life, needs, in greater or lesser degree,
the cooperation of the functions and activities of the spirit, that
is, of the intellect and imagination, as well as of the will; and he
who has more of these faculties and puts them to use, will succeed
in creating for himself a higher, broader and more vigorous life.
The difference between this creation and artistic creation consists
only in the fact that the former is *interested* and the latter *disinterested,* which explains why one is very common while the
other is not. Interested implies an objective of practical utility,
while disinterested means that its goal is within itself; the
former aims at obtaining something, while the latter wills itself
for itself. As a proof of this, we can quote the phrase "it was all
for the love of art," which we are accustomed to repeat whenever
bad luck, against all our expectations, has prevented us from at-
taining our own practical goals and interests. And the tone in
which this phrase is repeated explains why most people, who work
for utilitarian goals and do not understand the disinterested will,
are in the habit of calling the true poets mad, and the true poets
are those who experience artistic representation as it wills itself,
has itself as its only aim, and is willed by the poets exactly as it

wills itself. I shall not recall Cardinal Ippolito's query to Sir Lodovico Ariosto, who could have promptly answered merely by quoting from the canto of Astolfo's journey to the moon:

Non sí pietoso Enea, né forte Achille
fu, com'è fama, né sí fiero Ettorre;
e ne son stati e mille e mille e mille
che lor si puon con verità anteporre:
ma i donati palazzi e le gran ville
dai discendenti lor, gli ha fatto porre
in questi senza fin sublimi onori
dall'onorate man degli scrittori. (*Orlando furioso*, XXXV, 25)

(Aeneas was not as holy nor Achilles as strong
nor Hector as valiant as their fame proclaims;
there have been thousands upon thousands
who can in truth be classed ahead of them.
But the palaces and the great villas given
by their descendants have moved
the honored hands of writers
to lift them to such infinitely sublime honors.)

This shows how a feeling not thoroughly disinterested could blemish and mortify the work of even a very great poet. Fortunately this happened with regard to only one part of the poem. In a few other passages, one can observe that it is reflection rather than feeling that motivates the poetic representation which, when this happens, loses the spontaneous action of an organic and living being, and acquires a constrained and almost mechanical movement. It appears evident from those passages that the poet set out to comply with the serious norms of art in cold detachment; it is in these passages—as for instance, in the personifications of Melissa and Logistilla—where the poet's respect for the norms of art is no longer instinctive but deliberate.

But where his respect is indeed instinctive, does this result in a lack of irony? Is he then able to forget the unreality of his creation? And how does he identify with his world? These are the points that need clarification and require the most subtle analysis. Herein lies the secret of Ariosto's style.

*

In the distance of time and space, Ariosto beholds a marvelous world which was constructed around Charlemagne partly by legend and partly by the fanciful inventions of the poet-singers. He sees the Emperor no longer as Pulci's "dark thing" pacing the floor of the master chamber in fear of the formidable Saracen armies or, more frequently, in fear of the revenge that the Paladins were threatening over the treachery of Gano, who leads the Emperor by the nose as he pleases. Neither does he see him as Boiardo did, a doting Charles, who engages Angelica in lagging conversation, his face burning and his eyes aglow as he too has a craving for her. Ariosto realizes that such an emperor belongs to the world of farce or to the puppet theater. Let the people and children laugh at such puppets; it is easy to laugh when a figure is distorted in a grossly comical manner or when violence is somehow done to reality in a ludicrous way. This Ariosto cannot want, which is already enough reason not only to place him far above his predecessors, but perhaps to place him so far above them that—although he will then strive to lift the epic material to his own level even at the risk of going out of his wits—the material itself, because of a core of elements that have by now become permanently resistant to change, will remain partly too far beneath him. He dominates it as an absolute master, and, following the unpredictable whims of his wonderful creative fantasy, he combines and separates, puts together and sets apart all the elements with which it provides him. With this play, which is astonishing and captivating for its prodigious agility, he is able to save himself and his material. Wherever he can, in dealing with the eternal substance of human feelings and illusions, Ariosto identifies completely with his artistic world to the extent of giving it the very consistency of reality. But where he cannot do this, where the irreparable unreality of that world becomes evident to him, then he will give his representation an almost dream-like lightness, which is cheerfully kindled with a very subtle and pervasive irony, and which almost never breaks the spell that is cast by certain passages dealing with magic, nor does it break the much more wonderful spell that is exercised by the magic of his style.

There, I said the word: the magic of his style. The poet has realized that on one condition only could esthetic coherence and imaginative truth be given to that world, in which precisely magic plays such an important role: the condition that the poet become a magician himself and his style take its traits and virtues from magic. And there is the illusion which the poet creates in us and at times also in himself by identifying himself with his subtle playing to the extent of wholly surrendering himself to it. Oh, that play seems so beautiful to him that he would gladly believe it to be reality. Which it isn't, unfortunately; so much so that, from time to time, the fine veil tears open and thus exposes true reality, the reality of the present. When this happens, the thinly-spread irony gathers quickly and then suddenly bursts into view. But these bursts are never too unpleasantly harsh and never come as sudden shocks, because we have always anticipated them. And in addition to the illusions which the poet creates for us and for himself, there are those that the characters create for themselves and also those which the sorcerers and fairies create for them. It is all a phantasmagoric play of illusions, which does not so much involve the poetic world itself (as I have already mentioned, this representation often takes on the consistent aspect of reality), as it involves the style and the manner of representation adopted by the poet who, with remarkable perspicacity, has realized that only in this way, i.e., by competing with magic itself through his style, could he preserve the unalterable elements of his material and fit them coherently into the context of his poem. Do we want a proof of that? We can take canto XII where Ariosto competes with the magic arts of Atlante: the sorcerer has conjured up a castle, in which the knights exert themselves in a futile search for their women who they believe are being held prisoners there. Among the knights, Orlando, Ferraú and Sacripante are there looking for what they believe to be Angelica but is only her conjured form. At this point, Ariosto, much more of a magician than Atlante, brings Angelica, the real, living Angelica, into the castle, and furthermore enables her to become invisible— a trick that is a match for the empty form conjured up by Atlante.

Quivi entra, che veder non la può il mago;
e cerca il tutto, ascosa dal suo anello;
e truova Orlando e Sacripante vago
di lei cercar invan per quello ostello.
Vede come, fingendo la sua imago,
Atlante usa gran fraude a questo e a quello.
Chi tor debba di lor, molto rivolve
nel suo pensier, né ben se ne risolve.
. . . .
L'anel trasse di bocca, e di sua faccia
levò dagli occhi a Sacripante il velo.
Credette a lui sol dimostrarsi, e avvenne
ch'Orlando e Ferraú le sopravenne.
. . . .
Corser di par tutti alla donna, quando
nessun incantamento gl'impediva,
perché l'anel ch'ella si pose in mano
fece d'Atlante ogni disegno vano. (O. f., XII, 26, 28, 29)

(There she enters, hidden from the magician's eyes,
and, concealed by the ring, searches everywhere,
and finds Orlando and Sacripante, desirous
of her, searching through that mansion in vain.
She sees how Atlante feigns her image
and ingeniously deceives both of them.
She ponders for a long time which of the two to take,
and is not quite able to decide.

.   .   .   .

She took the ring from her mouth and showed
her face unveiled to Sacripante's eyes.
She thought she showed it to him alone but it happened
that Orlando and Ferraú unexpectedly came up to her.

.   .   .   .

They all ran together to the woman,
now that no enchantment held them back,
for the ring she placed in her hand
made all Atlante's plans vain.)

It is magic within magic. Ariosto knows how to make this device
serve his purpose; in fact, he employs it with such complete con-
fidence and mastery that within the span of a moment, as we
watch beguiled, reality becomes magic and magic becomes reality.
At the very moment when the real Angelica shows herself, reality
takes over and breaks the spell; she disappears by virtue of the
ring, and behold, Atlante's castle assumes a lifelike consistency
before our very eyes. How astonishingly subtle! It is a game of
magic, but what is truly magic is Ariosto's style.

What happens to those poor knights? "Volgon pel bosco or
quinci o quindi in fretta/ quelli scherniti la stupida faccia" (O.
f., XII, 36, "those scorned knights turn their blank faces/ here
and there through the forest, hastily"). What drives them to face
such mockingly deceptive situations and other worse troubles?
Love, of course, dear readers; and if love is not quite the same as
true madness, it is nonetheless the cause of so many of man's
follies, past, present, and future:

Chi mette il piè su l'amorosa pania,
cerchi ritrarlo, e non v'inveschi l'ale;
che non è in somma amor, se non insania,
a giudizio de' savi universale:
e se ben come Orlando ognun non smania,
suo furor mostra a qualch'altro segnale.
E quale è di pazzia segno più espresso
che, per altri voler, perder se stesso?

Varii gli effetti son, ma la pazzia
è tutt'una però, che li fa uscire.
Gli è come una gran selva, ove la via
conviene a forza, a chi vi va, fallire. (*O. f.*, XXIV, 1–2)

(He who sets his foot on the snare of love,
should draw it back and not get his wing in its lime,
for love is naught but a mad rage
by universal suffrage of the sages:
and albeit not all of us go crazy like Orlando,
his mad fury is shown by other signs.
And what sign of madness is more evident
than to destroy oneself for another?

Various are the effects, yet the madness
that causes them is all one.
It is like a great woods and
he who goes there must perforce lose his way.)

The last two lines convey a perfect idea of Ariosto's poem, which is based to a large extent on this love that makes people lose their mind. Enchanted fountains, gardens and castles? But of course! If to us moderns they are empty phantoms, they were close to reality in that remote world where Love made people do foolish things. You may laugh if you wish, but remember that Love, to man's scorn and torment, still creates today, and will continue to create tomorrow, more deceitful images with the perennial magic of its illusions. If you laugh at them, you may laugh at yourselves as well: "Frate, tu vai / l'altrui mostrando, e non vedi il tuo fallo" (*O. f.*, XXIV, 3, "Brother, you go on showing the errors of others, and do not see your own").

The truth is right beneath the surface of the fable. Look: the poet has only to force his hand slightly for the fable to turn into allegory. The temptation is strong, and occasionally he does yield to it, but luckily his fantasy lifts him again, at once, and calls him back to the right level and tone with which he had originally begun:

Dirò d'Orlando. . . .
che per amor venne in furore e matto,
d'uom che sí saggio era stimato prima;
se da colei che tal quasi m'ha fatto,
che 'l poco ingegno ad or ad or mi lima,
me ne sarà però tanto concesso,
che mi basti a finir quanto ho promesso. (*O. f.*, I, 2)

(Of Orlando I will tell. . . .
who through love became insane and mad
from a man who was judged so wise in former times;
if she, who has made me almost the same,
who constantly refined my small poetic wit,
will concede as much to me
as may suffice to fulfill what I promised.)

From the very beginning his style has the quality of magic. The entire first canto, in its manner of execution, is phantasmagoric, penetrated with flashes and fleeting apparitions. These flashes are intended to dazzle not only the readers but also the characters on the stage of the poem. Thus we have Rinaldo springing up in front of Angelica; Argalia in front of Ferraú who is searching for the helmet; Baiardo in front of Rinaldo; Angelica in front of Sacripante; Bradamante in front of Angelica and Sacripante; then comes the messenger, followed by Baiardo again, and finally Rinaldo again. And after an instantaneous flicker, these flashes vanish with the comic sense that results from the tricks of sudden deception. Ariosto employs this magic deliberately; he never gives the reader any time; he leaves one thing and picks up another; he bewilders and confuses both his readers and his characters, and then he laughs at that very bewilderment:

Non molto va Rinaldo, che si vede
saltare innanzi il suo destrier feroce:
"Ferma, Baiardo mio, deh, ferma il piede!
ché l'esser senza te troppo mi nuoce."
Per questo il destrier sordo a lui non riede,
anzi piú se ne va sempre veloce.
Segue Rinaldo, e d'ira si distrugge,
ma seguitiamo Angelica che fugge. (*O. f.*, I, 32)

(Rinaldo does not go too far before he sees
his fierce steed jump in front of him:
"Stop, Baiardo, stop your running,
for the loss of you is too harmful to me."
Still the deaf palfrey does not return
but keeps running with great speed.
Rinaldo chases him and is torn with rage,
but let us follow Angelica who flees.)

Imagine if Baiardo wanted to stop! His master is in love, which means he is mad. But "quel destrier, ch'avea ingegno a meraviglia" ("the steed who was endowed with an astonishing wit") understands what his master is unable to understand. Here is what happens: the good judgment that Love takes away from man is given by the poet to an animal. In the second canto Ariosto will say, by way of an additional remark, that the steed had "intelletto umano." Human indeed, but—let us understand one another—not of a man in love.

I would not really swear that there isn't some satire in this. Ariosto's irony is a very fine saw with a lot of sharp teeth, and, among them, that of satire, which cuts a little bit into everyone, beginning with his patron, Cardinal Ippolito, in a subtle and stealthy manner.

Oh gran bontà de' cavallieri antiqui! (*O. f.*, I, 22)

("Oh, the great generosity of the knights of old!")

Do you think that the irony of this passage consists merely in the fact that Ferraú and Rinaldo, after beating each other up in the manner you know, ride off together as if nothing had happened? Rajna says that numerous examples of such magnanimous courtesies, written in earnest, are already in the old French romances; he gives three examples from *Tristan,* and then concludes: "This is the courtesy and loyalty of the knights of England."[29] Very well! But it is not the same with Ariosto's two knights, who behave without a trace of chivalry. To see what I mean, let's imagine what Ferraú could have answered to Rinaldo's proposition that they suspend their duel: 'I do not fight for prey, but rather to defend a woman who calls for my help; if I have succeeded in defending her, I shall not have fought in vain.' This is what a good and truly noble knight of old would have answered. But both Rinaldo and Ferraú only look upon Angelica as prey to be taken possession of; and since she slipped out of their hands, they help each other find her with an attitude that is largely practical and scarcely chivalresque. Therefore, the exclamation "Oh, the great generosity of the knights of old!" is really ironic and has the ring of mockery, so much so that shortly after, in a similar situation of a duel being interrupted for the same reason, Rinaldo rides off, leaving Sacripante on foot:

E dove aspetta il suo Baiardo, passa,
e sopra vi si lancia, e via galoppa,
né al cavallier, ch'a piè nel bosco lassa,
pur dice a Dio, non che lo 'nviti in groppa. (*O. f.*, II, 19)

29 Rajna, p. 73. [tr.]

(He passes where his Baiardo was awaiting him,
jumps on him and gallops away;
to the knight, whom he leaves there on foot,
he doesn't even bid good-by, let alone invite him to ride on his horse.)

Now try to repeat in earnest, if you can: "Oh, the great generosity of the knights of old!"

The poet jests, and in the case of the poor king of Circassia, "that Sacripante tormented by love," the poet's jest is indeed cruel and goes too far. This was already present in his initial protrayal of him: "Un ruscello/ parean le guance, e 'l petto un Mongibello!" ("His cheeks looked like a flowing stream, and his chest a mountain like Mongibello.") The poet puts at his side the very woman— kindly and sympathetic—who makes him suffer.[30] Then, under Angelica's eyes, he has him pitifully thrown to the ground by a horseman who races by; Angelica has barely finished comforting him with subtle irony, that is, by blaming, as usual, the horse for his fall, when the poet subjects him to the final humiliation of hearing from a messenger who arrives galloping on a palfrey and looking troubled and exhausted:

Tu déi saper che ti levò di sella
l'alto valor d'una gentil donzella. (O. f., I, 69)

(You must know that the noble valor
of a gentle maid threw you from the saddle.)

A fatal blow for anybody, but it still isn't enough: here comes Rinaldo, Angelica flees, and poor Sacripante, king of Circassia, is left scorned, beaten, and on foot.

[30] It is really odd to note to what excessive lengths Rajna was led by his obsession to catch, at all costs, the poet of the *Orlando furioso* with his hand in someone else's bag. With respect to this episode of Sacripante and Angelica, he cites no fewer than twelve possible sources (pp. 74–85), but he doesn't realize that it is simply stupid to bring all these alleged sources together, for in Ariosto we find Angelica herself and not the usual knight who listens secretly to the laments of love. But Rajna has the courage to note that, while for Sacripante this is a difference of great moment, "for us, it is only secondary" (p. 80). Very well indeed! But this is like saying that, if Tasso, in presenting Clorinda's baptism, was really thinking of Sorgalis' baptism in *Chétifs,* the fact that Tancredi baptizes Clorinda instead of any other knight would only make a secondary difference. Now, do you know what Rajna considers to be the "substantial elements"? Grass, trees, water, if it is night or day, and other similar amenities. As if Angelica was not already in the woods from the beginning of the canto! Rajna should have spared himself such a display of erudition and should have merely taken up the episode of Prasildo in Boiardo. The difference however is still a substantial one. Ariosto takes this line from Boiardo: "che avria spezzato un sasso di pietade," and corrects it to read "che avrebbe di pietà spezzato un sasso." That's all there is to it.

But after all Sacripante can find consolation by realizing that such misfortunes do not happen to him alone. Even worse ones befall other people. There is enough for everyone. The poet amuses himself while giving form to the deceptiveness of the various illusions and in deceiving the very magicians who contrive the deceptions. It is a world at the mercy of love, magic, and fortune, so what do you expect? Of love, he shows the follies; of magic, he shows the deceptions; and, in the same way, of fortune, its mutability.

Ferraú, after parting from Rinaldo at the crossroads, goes on his way only to find himself "back at the starting point," and since he no longer expects to find Angelica, he forgets the beatings he gave and received and the delayed contest, and begins again to look for his helmet that had fallen into the water. Argalia, emerging from the waves holding the same helmet that Ferraú had dropped precisely where Argalia's body had been thrown, cries out to him:

Or se Fortuna (quel che non volesti
far tu) pone ad effetto il voler mio,
non ti turbare. . . . (O. f., I, 27)

(Now if Fortune makes good my wish
—something you did not want to do—
do not be troubled. . . .)

A passage which does not seem funny to us, but which perhaps was funny to those readers well acquainted with Boiardo's poem and characters, is the depiction of Ferraú's intense fright when, upon seeing Argalia's ghost, "ogni pelo *arricciossi*/ e *scolarossi* al Saracino il viso" ("the Saracen's hair curled from fright and his face lost all color"). Now Ferraguto had been portrayed by Boiardo as "tutto *ricciuto* e *ner* come carbone" ("all curly and as black as coal"). How could his hair become curled and his face discolored? Thus, is it not obvious that the poet is jesting here too?

The other antagonist, Rinaldo, sent by Charlemagne to England for reinforcements and thus distracted from his search for Angelica, "che gli avea il cor di mezzo al petto tolto" ("who had torn his heart from his breast"), arrived at Calesse the same day, and

contra la volontà d'ogni nocchiero,
pel gran desir che di tornare avea,
entrò nel mar ch'era turbato e fiero. (O. f., II, 28)

(Against the will of every pilot,
because he had a great desire to return,
he entered the sea that was troubled and hostile.)

But, yes indeed, pushed by the wind to the shores of Scotland, he forgets Angelica, forgets Charlemagne, forgets that he was in a great hurry to return, and goes deep into the Caledonian forests alone, changing from one path to another "dove piú aver strane avventure pensa" ("where he thinks he will meet more strange adventures"). And having come upon an abbey, first he eats, and then he asks the abbot where he could find those adventures through which he can show his bravery. And "the monks and the abbot":

Risposongli ch'errando in quelli boschi,
trovar potria strane avventure e molte:
ma come i luoghi, i fatti ancor son foschi;
che non se n'ha notizia le piú volte.
Cerca, diceano, andar dove conoschi
che l'opre tue non restino sepolte,
acciò dietro al periglio e alla fatica
segua la fama, e il debito ne dica. (O. f., IV, 56)

(They answered that, by wandering through those woods,
he could find many a strange adventure:
but, like the places, the deeds too are obscure,
for often one does not hear of them.
"Try," they said, "to go where you know
your deeds will not remain buried,
so that fame may follow after danger
and feats, and may tell of their due worth.")

Here Rajna is pleased to point out that "in all the Carolingian romances, never was there a baron converted so expediently into a knight-errant as in this case"; and he cannot help noticing that "the words of Rinaldo's hosts reveal nevertheless that the spirit of chivalry peculiar to medieval romances has by now vanished,"[31] because among the outstanding knights-errant modesty is always one of the very first obligations, so much so that nothing is so difficult as to induce them to acknowledge a certain glorious deed, and even when they perform before thousands of spectators, they contrive to conceal their identity behind an unknown coat-of-arms; they ride incognito most of the time, frequently changing insignias and often hiding their identity even from their closest and most loyal friends.

Shouldn't we deduce, therefore, that there is a satiric intention here and that furthermore this intention is so firmly resolute in Ariosto that it occasionally makes him neglect the serious norms

31 Rajna, p. 148. [tr.]

of art, which he usually respects more than all other writers? In fact, the esthetic inconsistency in Rinaldo's actions is quite obvious and inexcusable, for the character does not appear to be free but is rather subject to the author's intention.

I wanted to point this out because it seems to me that for some time now there has been a widespread tendency to force the extent to which a poet identifies with his material. Surely, it is difficult to see distinctly and precisely the limits of this identification. But those who, while rightfully recognizing the poet's identifying with his world, either deny the irony or largely exclude it or belittle its relevance, in my opinion, cannot even see those limits, or else their "light of understanding" is dim indeed. We need to recognize both elements—identification and irony—for the secret of Ariosto's style, I repeat, resides in the harmonious relationship that he makes of these apparently conflicting elements, a relationship which, although not always perfect, is nevertheless almost always achieved.

The poet's process of identification with his world consists in the fact that he, with his powerful imagination, *sees* as well carved out, or rather finished in all its forms, as precise, clearly-delineated, well-ordered, and alive, a world which others had assembled clumsily and had populated with beings so awkward, so ridiculous, so crudely inconsistent, and so on, that even their own authors could not take them seriously; a world also filled with wizards, fairies, and monsters which naturally increased its unreality and its unlikelihood. The poet lifts these beings out of their state as puppets and phantasms, and endows them with substance and consistency, vitality and character. Up to this point, he follows his own fantasy instinctively. Then the speculative faculty is introduced. As I have said before, there is in that world an irreducible element, an element, that is, that the poet fails to objectify seriously without showing that he is conscious of its unreality. With that astonishing device, which I mentioned earlier, he tries, however, to make it blend coherently with the whole. But his fantasy is not always helpful in this playful activity. And so he resorts to speculation: life loses its spontaneous movement and becomes a mechanical contrivance, an allegory. It is quite a strain. The poet strives to give a certain consistency to those fantastic constructions, which he senses have an irreducible unreality, by means of, let's say, a moral framework. It is a vain and misguided effort because the mere fact of giving an allegorical sense to a representation reveals clearly that the latter is already regarded as fable, devoid of both imaginative and real truth, and made up as a demonstration of a moral truth. One could confidently assert that the poet is not at all concerned with the demonstration of any moral truth and that those allegories were suggested to him by reflection, as a remedy. That was the world, and those were the elements that it made available. The element of magic and of the marvelous in chivalric poetry could in no way be eliminated without altering the fundamental nature of that world. And thus the poet either tries to reduce it to a symbol, or he simply accepts it, but, of course, with a sense of irony.

Even though a poet does not actually believe in the reality of his creation, he can still represent it as though he did believe in it, this is, by not showing in the least that he is conscious of its unreality; he can also represent as real a thoroughly fantastic dreamworld, which is regulated by its own laws, and which in the context of these laws is completely logical and consistent. When the poet creates with these conditions, the critic should no longer consider whether the artistic product is real or is a dream-world, but whether, as a dream-world, it is true: this is because the poet's intention was not to present an actual reality, but a dream having the appearance of reality, that is, of a reality which is dream-like, fantastic, and non-actual.

Now this is not the case with Ariosto. In more than one place, as we indicated earlier, he openly shows that he is conscious of the unreality of his creation. He also shows this when he gives a moral value and a logical (i.e., non-fantastic) coherence to the element of magic in that world. The poet does not want to create and represent a dream-world as true; he is not concerned only with the fantastic truth of his world, but also with its actual reality; he doesn't want his world to be inhabited by empty forms and puppets, but by men who are alive and real and who are affected and moved by our human passions. In short, the poet does not perceive the circumstances of that legendary past as having been converted into a fantastic reality through his artistic vision, but rather the reasons of the present carried to and embodied in that remote world. Naturally, when these reasons find, in that world, elements capable of accommodating them, the fantastic reality is saved; but when they do not find them, due to the unyielding resistance of those elements, then irony inevitably bursts out, and that reality is shattered.

What are these "reasons of the present"? They are the reasons of good sense, with which the poet is endowed; they are the reasons of life within the limits of natural possibility—limits which had been stupidly, crudely, and grotesquely abused, partly by legend, largely by the capriciousness of coarse and common poet-singers; they are, in a word, the reasons of the times in which the poet lives.

We saw Ferraú and Rinaldo riding together on the same horse, guided, as I said, by criteria that are largely practical and scarcely chivalresque; we heard the abbott's advice to Rinaldo who goes off in search of adventures; we could quote so many other examples, but it will suffice to discuss Ruggiero's flight on the hippogriff. Even when the poet succeeds, with the magic of his style, in giving the solid substance of reality to that marvelous element, as he then rises to an excessively high flight in this fantastic reality, all of a sudden, as though fearing that he or his listener might become dizzy, he plunges rapidly to the level of actual reality, thus breaking the spell of the fantastic reality. Ruggiero flies high on his hippogriff; but also from the sublime height of that flight the poet looks down and perceives on the ground the reasons of the present calling out to him to come down:

Non crediate, Signor, che però stia
per sí lungo cammin sempre su l'ale:
ogni sera all'albergo se ne gía,
schivando a suo poter d'alloggiar male. (O. f., X, 73)

(Do not believe, my Lord, that therefore
in so long a flight he was always on the wing:
every night he went to the inn
avoiding bad lodging as much as he could.)

And is this hippogriff real, actually real? In other words, does the poet present it without showing in the least that he is aware of its unreality? Ariosto sees it for the first time as it heads downwards from Atlante's castle in the Pyrenees, with the magician on its back, and he says that the castle, as such, was indeed not real, but invented, a work of magic; but not the hippogriff, the hippogriff was real and natural. Really? Was it actually real and natural? But of course it was, the offspring of a griffin and a mare, two animals which are native to the Rifei mountains. Is that so? Really? And how is it that we never see them? Well, they do come around, but *only once in a great while* . . . This last attenuating, clearly ironic, remark reminds me of that Neopolitan farce in which an impostor complains about his misfortunes, and, among other things, about that of his father who, for a number of months before dying, suffered a great deal as he was reduced, the poor man, to go on living without a liver. In answer to the observation that it is impossible to live without a liver, the impostor conceded that, yes, his father did have some liver left, but only a little bit, you see. The same thing can be said of the hippogriffs: they do show up, but only once in a great while! To be really taken for an impostor—this Ariosto does not want. It is as if he were saying: 'Dear readers, now, about these fables—I cannot really do without them; I must find a place for them in my poem, and I must show, as far as I can, that I believe in them.' As an example, here is the great wall that surrounds Alcina's city:

E par che la sua altezza al ciel s'aggiunga,
e d'oro sia da l'alta cima a terra. (*O. f.*, VI, 59)

(And it seems that its height reaches the sky
and that is gold from its tall summit to the ground.)

Now how can that be? A wall of that sort all made of gold?

Alcun dal mio parer qui si dilunga,
e dice ch'ell'è alchìmia; e forse ch'erra,
et anco forse meglio di me intende:
a me par oro, poi che sí risplende. (*O. f.*, VI, 59)

(Here someone dissents from my opinion
and says that it is alchemy; perhaps he is wrong,
and then maybe he understands better than I:
it seems gold to me, because it is so shiny.)

How can the poet put it better to you? He knows, as you do, that "all that shines is not gold," but it must appear to him as gold "because it shines like gold." In order *to be in tune* with that world as much as he can, he has declared himself, from the very beginning, to be mad like his hero. It is all a play of constant adjustments aimed at establishing the harmonious relationship between himself and his material, between the unlikely circumstances of that legendary past and the reasons of the present. He says:

Chi va lontan dalla sua patria vede
cose, da quel che già credea, lontane;
che narrandole poi, non se gli crede,
e stimato bugiardo ne rimane;
ché 'l sciocco vulgo non gli vuol dar fede,
se non le vede e tocca chiare e piane.
Per questo io so che l'inesperïenza
farà al mio canto dar poca credenza.

Poca o molta ch'io ci abbia, non bisogna
ch'io ponga mente al vulgo sciocco e ignaro.
A voi so ben che non parrà menzogna
che 'l lume del discorso avete chiaro. (*O. f.*, VII, 1–2)

(He who goes far from his native country sees
things different from what he believed before,
and later, in telling of them, is not believed,
and remains a liar in the opinion of others;
for the foolish crowd will not trust him
if clearly and plainly it does not see and touch them.
Therefore I know that inexperience will cause
my poem to gain little credence.

Whether I gain little or much of it, I need not
care about the foolish and ignorant crowd.
I am sure it will not appear a lie to you
whose light of understanding is clear.)

Here "aver chiaro il lume del discorso" means 'to know how to read through the thin surface of the verses.' This is the canto of Alcina, and here the poet's suggestion is: 'If I say Alcina, Melissa, or Erifilla, or if I say the *wicked* mob, Logistilla, Andronica, Fronesia, Dicilla, or Sofrosina, you will quite understand what I am referring to.' This is another (unfortunate) contrivance used to establish the aforementioned accord but which, like the other devices, also unveils the poet's irony, that is, his consciousness of the unreality of his creation. In places where this accord cannot be established, the irony, however, never bursts forth in a strident or discordant manner, precisely because the accord itself is always intended by the poet, and this intention is in itself ironic.

The irony resides in the vision the poet has not only of that fantastic world but of life itself and of man. Everything is fable and everything is true since it is inevitable that we accept as true the empty appearances emanating from our illusions and passions; to have illusions can be beautiful, but the deception of too much fantasizing always results in tears. This deception will appear to be comic or tragic depending on the degree of our involvement with the vicissitudes of those who suffer the deception, on the interest or sympathy which that passion or illusion arouses in us, and on the effects that the deception produces. Similarly we can see that the poet's ironic sense comes to the surface also in another aspect of the poem, and this time it does not stand out as obviously as before, but it shows itself through the artistic representation of the work in which it has transfused itself in a way that that representation feels and wants itself to be just the way it is. In short, the ironic sense, objectified, emerges from the artistic representation even in places where the poet does not openly show that he is aware of the unreality of that representation.

Here is Bradamante in search of her Ruggiero: to save him, she ran the risk of perishing at the hands of Pinabello from Maganza; the poet has her suffer, along with the readers, the torture of having to hear the enchantress Melissa foretell the whole line of her illustrious descendants, and having to see all of them pointed out to her by the enchantress. And then she sets off, she traverses inaccessible mountains, climbs precipices, crosses streams, reaches the sea, finds the inn where Brunello is staying (the poet does not say whether she eats there); and then again she takes to the road, "di monte in monte e d'uno in altro bosco" (O. f., IV, 11, "from mountain to mountain, from one woods to another"), until she arrives at the top of the Pyrenees; she gets the ring in her possession, fights with Atlante, succeeds in breaking the spell, makes the magician's castle vanish; and, yes indeed, after so much running, after so many hardships and torments, she has to see her Ruggiero, just liberated, being taken away from her by the hippo-griff. The only thing left for her is to receive compliments from those she had not intentionally planned to set free. But she doesn't even get that:

Le donne e i cavalier si trovâr fuora
de le superbe stanze alla campagna
e furon di lor molte a chi ne dolse,
ché tal franchezza un gran piacer lor tolse. (O. f., IV, 39)

(The ladies and knights found themselves
outside the proud halls and in the country;
and many were those who regretted it,
for such liberty deprived them of much enjoyment.)

Ariosto adds nothing more. A true humorist would not have let the astonishing opportunity slip by him of describing the effects produced upon knights and ladies by a sudden disenchantment, by finding themselves again in the country, and of describing the pain for the lost privilege of slavery in exchange for a liberty that awakens them from a pleasant dream and drops them into a bare and harsh reality. There is not even a hint of such a description in Ariosto. In its stead, the poet delights in offering another de-scription, just as Atlante amused himself in jesting with the knights that came to challenge him; I mean his comical description of the attempts by the liberated knights to get hold of the hippogriff, which leads them through the countryside,

come fa la cornacchia in secca arena,
che dietro il cane or qua or là si mena (*O. f.*, IV, 43)

(as does the crow on the dry sand,
which leads the dog here and there).

Why is the other description missing? Only because the poet has placed himself from the beginning, with respect to his material, in conditions completely opposite to those of a humorist. He avoids contrasts and seeks an accord between the reasons of the present and the fabulous situations of that remote world. He does achieve this harmony through irony for, as I have said, this intention to harmonize is in itself ironic. But the effect is that those conditions do not assert themselves as reality in the representation of the work; they dissolve themselves, as De Sanctis puts it, in irony, which destroys the contrast and therefore can no longer attain a comic dramatization, thus remaining comic but undramatic.

Instead, the reasons of the present assert themselves, as they are transported and infused into the elements of that remote world capable of accommodating them; and then we can have a dramatic result, but this will be seriously and even tragically represented, as in Guinevere, Olympia, and Orlando's madness. The two elements of the comic and the tragic never merge into one.

They will merge, however, in a work in which—far from showing that he is aware of the unreality of that fantastic world, far from seeking a harmonious accord with that world (an accord which by necessity is only possible through irony and after the awareness of that unreality has manifested itself in many ways), far from transferring to that fantastic world the reasons of the present by infusing them into the elements capable of accommodating them—the poet will give to that fantastic world of the past the substance of a living person, a body, and will call it Don Quijote, and will put into his mind and soul all those deceptive tales, and will set him in a continual and painful collision against the present. Painful in the sense that the poet, within himself, will feel his created character as alive and true and he will share his suffering from the conflicts and collisions.

For anyone seeking points of contact and similarities between

Ariosto and Cervantes, it would be enough simply to clarify in a few words the kind of situation in which Cervantes places his hero at the outset as compared to the situation in which Ariosto places himself. Contrary to Ariosto, Don Quijote does not pretend that he believes in that marvelous world of chivalric legends: he does in fact believe in it; he carries that world within himself; that world is his reality, his reason for being. The reality which Ariosto carries and feels within himself is quite different; it is as if, having this reality within himself, he were lost in the world of legend. As for Don Quijote, who has the legend in himself, it is as if he were lost in the real world. So much so that, in order not to be in a constant raving state and, as lost as they are, in order to find themselves somehow, one of them sets out to look for reality in legend, the other for legend in reality.

As one can see, these are two positions which are diametrically opposed. Don Quijote tells us: 'True, the windmills are windmills, but they are also giants. It is not that I, Don Quijote, mistook windmills for giants; but rather than Frestón changed the giants into windmills.' This is legend brought into the evident world of reality. Ariosto tells us: 'True, Ruggiero flies on the hippogriff. The enchanter Frestón—that is, the extravagant imagination of my predecessors—has stuck also animals such as this into our world; so I think it necessary for me to have my Ruggiero fly upon it: but let me assure you that every night he goes to an inn and does all he can to avoid being given bad lodging.' This is reality clearly evident in the world of legend.

Still, it is one thing to pretend to believe, and another to believe in earnest. That pretense, in itself ironic, can lead to an agreement with legend, which either dissolves in irony, as we have seen, or is allowed to change into the appearance of reality through a process contrary to the fantastic one, that is, by using a logical structure. On the other hand, true reality, if for a moment it allows itself to be changed into improbable forms by the fantastic contemplation of a madman, will resist and fight back if this madman, no longer satisfied only to contemplate it from a distance and in his way, comes close enough to clash against it. It is one thing to fight against an invented castle, which can suddenly be made to vanish, and another to fight against a real windmill, which does not let itself be struck down like an imaginary giant.

"Look, your grace," Sancho explains to his master, "those are not giants that have appeared there but windmills, and what seem to be their arms are really the sails which, turned by the wind, cause the millstone to rotate."[32] But Don Quijote turns his compassionate glance toward his pot-bellied squire and then shouts up to the windmills: "You may have more arms than Briareus to move around, but you still have me to pay." But alas, he is the one who ends up paying. And we laugh. But the laughter which suddenly erupts from this clash with reality is quite different from the one which arises in Ariosto's world as a result of the accord which the poet seeks to establish with that fantastic world by means of irony, which negates precisely the reality of that world. The latter is the laughter of irony while the former is the laughter of humor.

When Orlando also collides with reality, losing completely his senses, he throws away his weapons, removes his masks, strips himself of the whole legendary apparatus, and, a naked man, falls headlong into reality. The result is tragedy. No one can laugh at his appearance or his actions and whatever comic quality they may have is surpassed by the tragic force of his fury. Also Don Quijote is mad, but he is a madman who does not bare himself; on the contrary, he is a madman who clothes himself, who puts on legendary apparatus, and thus disguised, sets off in all seriousness to seek his ridiculous adventures.

The former's nakedness and the latter's use of disguise are the most evident signs of their madness. In Orlando's tragic nature there is a comic element; in Don Quijote's comic nature there is a tragic element. We, however, do not laugh at the frenzied actions of that naked man; we laugh at the valiant deeds of the man disguised, but we also feel that whatever tragic element he has is not completely nullified by the comicality of his masking, whereas the comicality of the other's nakedness is nullified by the tragic character of his enraged passion. In short, we feel that in Don Quijote the comic is also surpassed, not however by the tragic, but rather through the comic sense itself.[33] We pity while laughing, or we laugh while pitying.

How did the poet succeed in achieving this effect?

[32] Cervantes, *Don Quijote*, Chap. VIII. [tr.]

[33] I am using here Lipps' formula of humor as "the sublimation of the comic through the comic sense itself" (*Komik und Humor*, p. 243). What exactly does that mean? The explanation that Lipps gives does not seem acceptable to me for the same reasons that invalidate his whole esthetic theory. See Croce's criticism of that theory in his *Estetica*, Part II, p. 434.

*

As far as I am concerned, I cannot convince myself that the ingenious knight Don Quijote was born "in a place in La Mancha" rather than in Alcalá de Henares in 1547. I cannot convince myself that the famous battle of Lepanto, which, like so many magnanimous chivalric undertakings spectacularly prepared, was to come to naught, so much so that the astute Grand Vizier of Selim could say to the Christians: "We have cut off one of your arms by taking the island of Cyprus from you; but what have you done to us by destroying so many of our ships that were promptly rebuilt? You have cut off our beards, which grew back the next day!"—I cannot convince myself, as I was saying, that the famous battle of Lepanto, from which the Christian allies failed to derive any advantage, is not somewhat like "the frightening and never-before imagined adventure of the windmills."

"This, Sancho," says Don Quijote to his faithful squire, "this is a good war, and it is a great service to God to eliminate such bad seed from the face of the earth" (Chap. VIII). Did Don Quijote then not see Turkish turbans on the heads of those giants, which to the good Sancho appeared to be windmills?

Perhaps, for Spain, they were windmills. The island of Cyprus was a matter of concern for the Venetian lords, and a war against the Turks could be a matter of concern for Pius V, the proud Dominican pope, in whose aging veins was still stirring the hot blood of youth. But, during those beautiful spring days when Torres arrived in Spain, where he had been sent by the Pope to plead the Venetians' cause, Philip II was on his way to the lavish festivities of Cordova and Seville: the Grand Vizier's ships—windmills!

But not for Don Quijote: I mean for the Don Quijote, not of La Mancha, but of Alcalá. In his eyes, they were real giants, and with what a giant's heart did he set out to fight them.

Unfortunately, it went badly for him. But he refused to submit to the evidence, just as he refused to submit to any enemy or to his cruel luck. He said then that the vicissitudes of war, more than any other, are subject to continual change. He believed, and it seemed to him to be true, that the wicked enchanter, his enemy, the magician Frestón, the one who had dispossessed him of his books and house, had turned the giants into windmills in order to rob him even of the honor of victory. Only of this? The wicked magician took away his left hand as well. His hand, and then his liberty.

Many people have inquired into how it happened that Miguel Cervantes de Saavedra, the courageous soldier, the veteran of Lepanto and Terceira, succeeded in creating a character like the Knight of the Mournful Countenance and in composing a book like *Don Quijote,* rather than sing in epic form—as would have been more in keeping with his heroic nature—the Cid's exploits, the victories of Charles V, the battle of Lepanto itself, or the expedition to the Azores. And some people have even held the notion that Cervantes created his hero for the same reason that our good Tassoni later created his Count of Culagna. There were others, it is true, who went so far as to say that the real reason for the work lies in the conflict, always present in us, between the poetic and prosaic tendencies of our nature, and between our dreams of generosity and heroism and the harsh experiences of reality. But this reason, which would be, at best, an abstract explanation of the book, does not tell us why it was written.

All the critics, more or less, having rejected as untenable Sismondi's and Bouterwek's views, have accepted what Cervantes himself affirms both in the prologue of Part One of his masterpiece and at the end of Part Two: that is, that his book has no other aim than that of putting an end to books of chivalry and of destroying the importance they have in the world and among the common people, and that the author's only desire was to leave it up to his reader to denounce the false and extravagant tales of chivalry which, since they have been mortally wounded by the story of his own true *Don Quijote,* can no longer walk but stagger along and are doubtlessly bound to collapse.

Now we should be careful not to contradict the author himself, especially since it is well known how much influence was exerted by books of chivalry at that time in Spain, and how the taste for this literature had reached the level of madness. Rather we shall profit from these words and we shall make use of the author and the story of his life in demonstrating the true reason for the book and the reason, which is more profound, for its humor.

How did the idea originate in Cervantes to extract his hero, alive and real, from his own land and time, rather than from the far away France of Charlemagne's time, and to exalt him with the purpose expressed in the words of the prologue? When and where did the idea come to him, and why?

There is good reason for the extraordinary reception given to the epic and to chivalric literature during that time; the struggle between Christianity and Islam was the nightmare of Cervantes' century. And the poet, who since his early years had been under the spell of the spirit of chivalry as the poor but proud descendant of a noble family that for many centuries was devoted to the monarchy and to arms, was all of his life an ardent defender of the faith. There was therefore no need for him to go far off into legend to seek his hero, a knight who stood for faith and justice: he had this man present in himself. And this hero fights in Lepanto; as a slave in Algiers, this hero stands up for five years to Hassan, the cruel Berber king; this hero fights in three other campaigns for his king against the French and the English.

How does it happen that suddenly these campaigns are changed into windmills and the helmet that he was wearing into a cheap barber's basin?

One of Sainte-Beuve's notions has had wide acceptance, to wit, that in great works of the human spirit there is concealed a future *plus-value*, which develops by itself, independently of the authors themselves, just as the flower and the fruit develop from the seed without the gardener's having done anything but skillfully tilled, raked, and watered the soil, and having finally given it all the care and substances that best make it fertile. This notion would have been very useful to all those scholars who during the Middle Ages discovered innumerable allegories in Greek and Latin poets. This was also another way of dissolving the work of art into logical patterns. It is true that when a poet is genuinely successful in giving life to one of his characters, this character lives independently of its author, so much so that we can imagine it in other situations in which the author never intended to place it, and see it behave according to its own inner laws—laws which not even the author would have been able to violate; it is true that this character, in which the author was instinctively successful in gathering, unifying, and vivifying so many individual characteristics and so many random elements, can later become what is usually called a "type," something that was not a part of the author's intention at the moment of creation.

But can this really be said of Cervantes' *Don Quijote?* Can one say and seriously maintain that the author's intention in writing his book was solely to obliterate, using ridicule as his weapon, all the authority and prestige that the books of chivalry had established in the world and among the common people, in order to eliminate their harmful effects? And can one equally maintain that the author never dreamed of putting in his masterpiece all that we see in it?

Who is Don Quijote, and why is he considered mad? After all —and this is recognized by everybody—he has but a single sacred aspiration: justice. He wants to take up the cause of the oppressed, overthrow the oppressors, provide a remedy for the wrongs of fate, avenge the violent deeds wrought by evil. How much more beautiful and noble life would be, how much more just the world, if only the aims of the ingenious knight could successfully be carried out! Don Quijote is a gentle person, has exquisite feelings, is generous and neglectful of himself, totally devoted to the welfare of others. And how well he speaks! What frankness and generosity in everything he says! He considers sacrifice a duty, and all his actions, at least in intent, are deserving of praise and gratitude.

Where then is the satire? We all are fond of this virtuous knight. If on the one hand his misfortunes make us laugh, on the other hand they move us deeply.

If Cervantes intended therefore to demolish the books of chivalry because of their harmful effects on the minds of his contemporaries, the example that he creates in Don Quijote does not carry out his intentions. The effect produced by those books on Don Quijote is disastrous only for him, that is, for the poor *hidalgo*. And it is disastrous only because the idealism of chivalry could no longer be made to conform with the reality of the new times.

Now this is precisely what Miguel Cervantes de Saavedra had learned at his own expense. How had he been rewarded for his heroism, for the two harquebus wounds he received and the loss of his hand in the battle of Lepanto, for the five years of slavery endured in Algiers, for his bravery demonstrated in the assault on Terceira, for his nobility of spirit, for the greatness of his poetic genius, for his patient modesty? What had become of his noble dreams that had impelled him to go to war and to write immortal pages? What had become of his radiant aspirations? He had become a knight like his Don Quijote, he had entered into battle, facing enemies and risks of all kinds for just and holy causes, he had always had the sustenance of the most lofty and noble ideals, and what had been his rewards? After struggling to make a miserable living in positions unworthy of him, he was first excommunicated while serving as commissary of military supplies in Andalusia, and then, swindled while a tax-collector, did he not end up in prison? And where was that prison? In a place, the very place, called La Mancha. In a dark and run-down Manchegan prison, *Don Quijote* was born.

But the real Don Quijote had been born before: he had been born in Alcalá de Henares in 1547. He had not yet found out who he was, he had not yet seen himself in full light: he had believed that he was fighting against giants and that he was wearing Mambrino's helmet. There, in the dark Manchegan prison, he recognizes himself, he finally *sees himself*. He becomes aware that the giants were windmills and Mambrino's helmet a cheap barber's basin. He sees who he is and laughs at himself. All his sufferings burst into laughter. Oh, what a fool! What a fool! Yes, burn them at the stake, all the books of chivalry!

This is something quite unlike the future *plus value*! Read what Cervantes says to the idle reader in the prologue to Part One: "But I have not been able to contravene the natural order for in it *each thing engenders its likeness*. Thus, what could my sterile and poorly cultivated mind engender but the story of an emaciated, shrivelled, capricious offspring, filled with varied and never-before imagined thoughts, much like the one that was engendered in a jailhouse, where every discomfort resides and every sad sound makes its abode?"

How else could one explain the deep bitterness which, like a shadow, follows each step, each ridiculous act, each wild adventure that the poor Manchegan knight undertakes? It is the sense of grief that inspires the very image in the author when, substantiated as it is with his suffering, it wills itself as funny. And it wills itself so because reflection, the product of the most bitter experience, has suggested to the author the *feeling of the opposite*, through which he recognizes his error and he wants to punish himself with the mockery that others will make of him.

Why didn't Cervantes sing of the Cid Campeador? Who knows if in the dark and dilapidated prison the image of that hero did not actually come to him and arouse in him an anguishing envy! Between Don Quijote—who wished to live in his time, not really as the knights-errant had lived in their time, but rather as they had lived outside of time and out of the world, in the legend or in the reverie of poets—and the Cid Campeador who, helped by his time, succeeded in converting his personal history into legend, did not a dialogue take place in that prison, in the presence of the poet?

Among the other peoples, the chivalric romance created its own fictitious characters, or, to put it more accurately, this romance came out of the legend which had formed around the knights. What happens then to that legend? It grows, transforms, idealizes; it abstracts from common reality, from the substance of life, from all the ordinary events that create life's greatest hardships. In order for a personage—and now we are speaking not of a fictitious character but of a man who takes as his model the immeasurable ideal images formed by the collective imagination or by a poet's fantasy—to be able successfully to infuse his own life into these grandiose legendary masks, what is required is not only an extraor dinary greatness of soul, but also the help of his time. This happened in the case of the Cid Campeador.

But Don Quijote? He has the bravery to meet every test, a very noble spirit, the flame of faith; that bravery however only begets him humiliating beatings; that noble spirit is simple madness; and the flame of his faith is a paltry wick that the knight obstinately persists in keeping lit, a defective, patched-up balloon that fails to rise, that has illusions of attacking the clouds, in which it sees giants and monsters, and yet it moves close to the ground, tripping up on all the underbrush, broken branches, and sharp rocks, which lacerate it miserably.

Chapter VI.   ITALIAN HUMORISTS

It is not my intention to trace even the barest outline of the history of humor in the Latin countries and particularly in Italy. My only intention, in the first part of this book, is to refute those who have tried to maintain, on the basis of certain preconceptions and certain divisions and considerations, that humor is a wholly modern phenomenon and an almost exclusive prerogative of the Anglo-Germanic peoples. As I think I have demonstrated, such divisions are arbitrary and such considerations too general.

If my discussion of those divisions and considerations has prevented me from proceeding as quickly as I had planned, detaining me while I closely observed certain aspects and conditions in the history of Italian literature, it has not however diverted me at all from the principal subject—a subject which requires moreover to be treated with subtle penetration and minute analysis. I have gone around it, but with the sole purpose of gradually encompassing and better penetrating it from all angles.

If there is someone who thinks that he has found a contradiction between my subject and the examples of Italian writers cited thus far as writers in whom I do not find the note of *true* humor, I shall remind him that I said at the beginning that there are two ways of understanding humor, and that precisely in this lies the real crux of the question: namely, if humor should be understood in the broad sense in which it is usually understood, and not only in Italy, or in a more restricted and specialized sense, with its own well-defined characteristics, which in my opinion is the proper way of understanding it. Taken in the broad sense, I have said, humor can be found in great abundance both in ancient and modern literatures; taken in the restricted sense, in my view the right one, it will likewise be found among modern and ancient writers of all countries, although in much smaller quantities and only in a *very few exceptional works,* since it is not a prerogative of any particular nation or any particular age, but rather the result of a very special natural disposition, of a deep psychological process which can occur just as well in a wise man of ancient Greece, like Socrates, as in a poet of modern Italy, like Alessandro Manzoni.

However, it is not right to take, according to one's fancy, either one of the two points of view and to apply the first to a particular literature only to conclude that no humor is to be found there, and to apply the second to another literature only to demonstrate that humor is native to it. It is not right, because of the difference among languages, that the Italians should sense that particular flavor only in foreign writers—a flavor which, due to the familiarity that we have with our own means of linguistic expression, we no longer perceive in the Italian writers, whereas the foreigners, in turn, do perceive it in them. In doing this, we Italians will end up being the only ones to deny any trace of humor to Italian literature, while the English, for example, will be seen placing in the forefront of their literature a humorist like Chaucer, who at best can be considered a humorist only if one takes humor in its wider sense, namely, the sense in which also Boccaccio, together with many other Italian writers, can be considered a humorist.

So there is no contradiction on our part. The contradiction is, instead, on the side of those who, after affirming that humor is a Nordic phenomenon and a prerogative of Anglo-Germanic peoples, mention Rabelais and Cervantes, a Frenchman and a Spaniard, when they wish to cite two admirable examples of the most complete and genuine humor; or they mention Rabelais and Montaigne; and when they mention Rabelais, they are incapable of seeing, in their own house, Pulci, Folengo, and Berni; and when they mention Montaigne—who is the type of serene skeptic, reluctant to struggle, smiling, restrained, with no ideal to defend nor the strength to persist, the skeptic who tolerates everything and has faith in nothing, who has neither enthusiasm nor aspirations, who uses doubt to justify inertia through tolerance, who shows a perception of the serene but sterile life, a clear sign of selfishness and decadence of race (since the free inquiry which does not encourage action is more apt to accept, and to become an accomplice of, despotism than to save anyone from slavery)—they do not perceive, I repeat, that the reasons for which they deny to so many Italian writers not only the particular feature of humor but also the possibility of their ever having it, are precisely the reasons which they claim have produced Montaigne's humor. As one can see, this is like having one scale but two standards of measure.

We shall see that, actually, having a profound belief, an ideal goal, having an aspiration and struggling to attain it, far from being conditions necessary to humor, are rather obstacles to it; and yet the person who has a belief, an ideal goal or an aspiration, and who struggles in his own way to achieve it, he, too, can be a humorist. In short, any such ideal, in itself, does not dispose anyone to humor but rather works as a handicap against it. But still the writer may well have an ideal, and when he does, humor, which stems from other causes, will certainly be affected by it, just as it will be affected by all the other traits of the temperament of a certain humorist. In other words: humor does not require an ethical basis; it may or may not have one: this depends on the personality, on the temperament of the writer; but naturally, the presence or the lack of it will result in humor having different qualities and producing different effects, that is, in its being more or less bitter, more or less harsh, in its inclining more or less towards tragedy or comedy, or towards satire or burlesque, etc.

People who believe that it is all a play of contrasts between the poet's ideal and reality, and who maintain that if that ideal is bitterly thwarted and scorned by reality, the result will be invective, irony, or satire; that if the poet is only slightly irritated by reality or if the contrast between the appearances of reality and himself causes him to laugh more or less heartily, then the result will be comedy, farce, jest, caricature, or the grotesque; and that finally humor will result if the poet's ideal does not become offended and does not react with indignation, but rather compromises good-naturedly, with a somewhat painful indulgence—these people show that they have an excessively one-sided and somewhat superficial view of humor. It is true that a great deal depends on the poet's temperament and that his ideal, confronted by reality, may react with indignation, or laughter, or compromise; but an ideal that compromises does not really show that it is sure of itself and profoundly rooted. And is this limitation of the ideal all that humor consists of? Not at all. The limitation of the ideal, if anything, would be not the cause but rather the result of the particular psychological process which is called humor.

Let us therefore forget, once and for all, about ideals, faith, aspirations, and so forth: the skepticism, tolerance, and realistic character, which Italian letters acquired almost from their beginning, were certainly dispositions and conditions favorable to humor; the greatest obstacle was the dominating rhetoric, which imposed abstract rules and norms of compositions, a purely *mental* literature, almost mechanically constructed, in which the subjective elements of the spirit were stifled. Once the yoke of this intellectualistic literary practice was broken, we said, by the rebellion of precisely the subjective elements of the spirit, which characterizes the Romantic movement, humor asserted itself freely, especially in Lombardy, which was the battlefield of Italian Romanticism. But this so-called Romanticism was the last clamorous call to arms of the will and of the emotions rebelling against the intellect. In many other periods, in many other moments of the literary history of every country, such rebellions occurred; and there have always been rebellious spirits acting alone, and there have always been the common people who express themselves in their various dialects without having learned rules and laws in school.

It is among these solitary writers who rebelled against rhetoric, and among these people who wrote in dialect that we must look for the humorists; and if we take humor in its wider sense, we shall find many humorists from the very beginning of Italian literature, especially in Tuscany. If we take humor in its true sense, we shall find few humorists among the Italians, but surely we will not find more of them in the literature of other countries, nor can it be said that the few Italian humorists are inferior to the few foreign ones with whom we are, to our confusion, constantly presented, and who, if we take a close look, are always the same and can be counted on the fingers of one hand. Only that, concerning the value and flavor of Italian humorists, we have never been capable of bringing these qualities to the fore and appreciating them, nor have we ever been capable of recognizing and duly distinguishing them, because Italian critics and literary historians, guided in their work by prejudices that have nothing to do with esthetics or, in any case, guided by generalizations, have failed to yield to flexibility and adjust to each particular instance, and have judged as errors, exaggerations, and faults what were instead their special characteristics. I only wonder what kind of appraisal would we find in Italian literary histories of a book like *The Life and Opinions of Tristram Shandy* if it had been written in Italian by an Italian; I wonder what masterpieces of humor such as, let's say, *Circe* and *I capricci del bottaio* (and perhaps even Gian Carlo Passeroni's *Vita di Cicerone*) would be if they had been written in English by an English writer.

A few years ago I was mentioning this very point to a highly cultivated Englishman, who had a profound knowledge of Italian literature. "Not even in Machiavelli?" he asked me in astonishment, as if he couldn't believe it. "You mean to say that not even in Machiavelli do Italian critics recognize humor? Not even in the short story about Belfagor?"

And I was thinking about the pure greatness of this eminent Italian writer, who never dressed out of the wardrobe of rhetoric; who was among the very few who understood the power of things; who always based his logic on facts; who always reacted with the most keen-witted and subtle analyses against all confused syntheses; who dismantled all ideal contrivances with two tools, experience and argumentation; who demolished with laughter every exaggeration of form. I was thinking that no one had a greater intimacy of style nor a keener sense of observation; that few temperaments were endowed with Machiavelli's natural ability to perceive the conflicts of life and to be so profoundly affected by the impact of its incongruencies. I was thinking that—as to many people a characteristic of humor is a concern for details together with what, "to judge on an abstract level and from first impression," D'Ancona calls a kind of "triviality and vulgarity"[1]—he too, Machiavelli, mixed with the common herd even as low as the level of vulgarity, and to the point where he himself wrote: "So trapped among these lice, I scrape the mold from my wits and work off this malevolence of my lot, content that it trample me in this way, anxious to see if it should feel some shame for it";[2] but he also wrote:

Però se alcuna volta io rido o canto,
facciol perché non ho se non quest'una
via da sfogare il mi' angoscioso pianto.[3]

(And thus if I sometimes laugh or sing,
I do it because this is the only way for me
to ease my painful grief.)

I was thinking also of De Sanctis' perceptive remark that "Machiavelli employs the tolerance that understands and absolves; not the indifferent tolerance of the skeptic, of the dull-minded, of

[1] Alessandro D'Ancona, *Studi di critica e storia letteraria* (Bologna: Zanichelli, 1880), p. 180. [tr.]

[2] N. Machiavelli, Letter of December 10, 1513, to Francesco Vittori, in *Opere* (Milan, Naples: Ricciardi, 1954), p. 1110. [tr.]

[3] *Ibid.*, Letter of April 16, 1513, to Francesco Vittori; the verses cited are after Petrarch, *Rime*, 70. [tr.]

the fool, but the tolerance of the man of science who doesn't hate the matter he analyzes and studies, and treats it with the irony of the man who stands above his passions and says: I tolerate you, not because I approve of you, but because I understand you."[4] I was thinking about all of these elements which, if we made a list of them, quite intentionally now, are precisely those the experts of foreign literatures recognize as characteristic of the true and most celebrated humorists (English and German, of course!), and —may God forgive me—I no longer knew whether to laugh or cry at all the marvels that these experts have always said about, let's say, Dean Jonathan Swift's *The Drapier's Letters* and other political writings.

To these experts, who always hold up to us the usual five or six humorous writers selected from foreign literatures, it will suffice to give an appraisal of Italian literature like the following:

The work of art is an ingenious play of fantasy; a fleeting laughter, impressional in nature and awakened by images and not by things; academic joy of memories, scholarly gaiety. It lacks the profound feeling of the family [*and surely Swift had so much of this!*], of nature, of one's homeland; or rather, it lacks them in that cheerful form and assumes a form which is bitter and violent [*and what honey, in fact, Swift has!*], which reminds us of Persius and Juvenal. I shall not mention names; it will suffice to point out that just as other obstacles, such as the Papacy, foreign domination, internal discords, regional arrogance, the academies and schools, hindered political, religious, and scientific liberty, so too has the classical traditions, the spirit of imitation, the language restricted in vocabulary and aloof from the people, obstructed, in art, the freedom of attitudes, form and style which is indispensable to humor. We suffer from an ancient ill: we are pedantic in science, rhetorical in art, solemn or serious actors in life, intolerant of analysis, easily taken by broad ideas, scornful of modest and slowly-maturing experiences, searchers of thesis and antithesis, vague or empirical thinkers, atheists or mystics, sophisticated or barbaric. Our culture is made up of different strata, and is not always indigenous; the foreigner is still within us; literary forms have fixed types; one generation composes a text, several succeeding ones annotate it. Thus our people think and feel by reflex, by reminiscence, or by pure fantasy. The real meaning of life escapes us and the freedom of perception and attitudes that creates humor becomes deadened. All this reactivates the vicious circle: humorists do not emerge on account of the lack of suitable conditions; conditions do not change because of the lack of humorists. The defect is at the foundation: our spirit of curiosity is underdeveloped and our inner zest is feeble. Humor requires both these qualities: it requires the thinker and the artist; but

---

[4] Francesco De Sanctis, *Scritti varii inediti o rari* (Naples: Morano, 1898), II, 16. [tr.]

among us, art and learning are separated from each other, and both are severed from life.[5]

I already quoted Machiavelli. I shall quote, in this connection, another insignificant Italian writer who did not have the "freedom of attitudes, form and style which is indispensable to humor," and whose political, religious, and scientific liberty was "obstructed" by the Papacy, the academies, and the schools; a man intolerant of analysis, pedantic in science, rhetorical in art; a man whose spirit of curiosity was not developed, etc.: Giordano Bruno, who was, if you will, *an academic member of no academy,* and the author, among other things, of *Spaccio de la bestia trionfante, Cabala del cavallo pegaseo, Asino cillenico,* and *Candelaio;* a man whose motto, as everyone knows, was *In tristitia hilaris, in hilaritate tristis* ("Merry in sadness, sad in merriment"), which seems the motto of humor itself.

The candle of that *Candelaio* of his, the author says, "will be able to shed some light on certain *shadows of the ideas,* which truly frighten the beasts"; and he also says: "Consider the comings and goings, what people do, what they say, how it is understood, how it can be understood; for if you observe these human actions and conversations with Heraclitus's or Democritus's understanding, you will have the occasion either to laugh or to cry a great deal."

For his part, the author has contemplated them with the understanding of both Heraclitus and Democritus:

Here Giordano speaks in the common language; he names things freely; he gives the proper names to those to whom nature gives the proper beings; he does not call shameful that which nature makes worthy; he does not cover what nature shows openly; he calls bread, bread; wine, wine; the head, head; the foot, foot, and the other parts by their own names; he calls eating, eating; sleeping, sleeping; drinking, drinking, and likewise designates all other natural acts with their own names.

That is what he says in the "Epistola esplicatoria" to the *Spaccio de la bestia trionfante* ("Expulsion of the triumphant beast"). Now let us open the *Spaccio* itself and let us hear what Mercury says of Jupiter:

He has ordered that today, at noon, two melons, among the others in Fronzino's melon patch, shall reach the peak of ripeness, but that they shall not be picked until three days later, when they will be judged

[5] Giorgio Arcoleo, *L'umorismo nell'arte moderna.* Due conferenze al Circolo filologico di Napoli (Naples: Detken, 1885), pp. 94–95.

unfit to eat. He demands that, at the same time, thirty jujubes shall be gathered, perfectly ripened, from the jujube tree, which is at the foot of Mt. Cicala, on Gioan Bruno's land; that seventeen, still unripe, shall fall to the ground, and that fifteen shall be worm-eaten; that Vasta, Albenzio's wife, while trying to curl the hair on her temples, having overheated the iron, shall singe fifty-seven strands of her hair without however burning the skin, and that she shall not curse this time upon smelling the stench of burned hair, but rather shall endure it patiently; that out of the dung of Albenzio's ox, two hundred and fifty-two beetles shall be hatched, of which fourteen shall be trampled and killed by Albenzio's foot, twenty-six shall die from *rinversato* [a vinegar insecticide], twenty-two shall live in a cave, eighty shall wander about the courtyard, forty-two shall go to live under the tree stump near the door, sixteen shall keep rolling their little dung balls around wherever they see fit, and the rest shall run to chance . . . He decreed that Ambruoggio, in his one-hundred and twelfth thrust, shall finally carry out and conclude the business with his wife, and that he shall not impregnate her this time but shall do so another time, with the semen into which the cooked leek is converted that he is presently eating with millet bread and grape jam.[6]

And this is to show Sofia that she is mistaken if she believes that the gods are not concerned with the smallest things as well as with the greatest ones. What do we call this?

Here is how Bruno describes himself in the first preface to *Candelaio:*

If you knew the author, you might say that he has a bewildered look; it seems that he is constantly contemplating the sufferings of hell; he gives the impression of having been put through a press like a metal bar; a person who laughs only to do as other people do. You will see him irritated, hesitant, eccentric: he is never happy with anything, as shy as an eighty-year old man, capricious like a dog.

In the prefatory epistle to the *De l'infinito universo et mondi,* he refers to himself as Dedalus, "with respect to his habits of intellect," and in the *Spaccio* he introduces himself as Momo, the god of laughter.

In his admirable study on three Italian comedies of the sixteenth century, Arturo Graf says:

Bruno's style is the vivid image of the mind from which it emanates. A great variety of forms, images, and techniques is matched by an incomparable effectiveness of style. Bursting with the fervor of life, his style does not rest upon the symmetrical compartments of traditional rhetoric but rather it develops through a flowing and organic process. Everchanging in nature, it adapts with equal flexibility to the most arduous idea of a disquisitive mind, and to the most vulgar sentiment of an abject soul.

---

[6] Giordano Bruno, *Spaccio,* I, 3. [tr.]

Words confront each other in unexpected encounters, and from their clash new ideas erupt in a dazzling light. Bruno's style is alive, fermenting with rare conceits, epiphaneous images, fertile insights. The language is richly endowed to match the great number and variety of things which must find expression through language, and it either is ignorant of, or flaunts the restraints and laws of, academic purity and enriches itself with elements taken not only from the most venerable repositories of classical eloquence but also from the most intimate recesses of the spoken language. Such an instrument was indispensable to a genius which, without ever losing its balance, is capable of grasping all the levels of being, from the lowest depths of reality to the loftiest planes of the ideal world. Whether it confronts, associates, or takes apart the elements of thought, or whether it narrates or describes, Bruno's style always maintains its unique character.[7]

The undeniable contradictions that Graf discovers in the pantheist philosopher's mind and that compel him to confess that he fails to understand "how the moment of laughter originates in that mind" are perfectly explained, in my opinion, by the inner and special psychological process which is exactly what humor consists of and which, in itself, implies these and many other contradictions. Besides, Graf himself adds that "it may be that the contradiction stems from a certain pre-existent discrepancy between his intellect and his temperament on one hand, and between his faculty of perception and his faculty of ratiocination on the other."

I cannot take the time, of course, to talk about every writer

[7] Arturo Graf, in *Studii drammatici* (Turin: Loescher, 1878); the three plays are *La calandria, La mandragola,* and *Candelaio.* Some of Bruno's figures of speech are without parallel in expressiveness as, for example, when he says of an inept speaker that he came armed with "words and sayings that are dying from hunger and thirst." Certain comparisons stand out sharply as when he says of two conceited wise men that "one seemed the constable of the ogre's giant wife and the other seemed the sheik of the goddess Reputation." And here is how Bruno describes the soothsayer-philosopher Don Cocchiarone in his *Cabala del cavallo pegaseo:* "The most reverend Don Cocchiarone, full of infinite and noble wonder, walks back and forth the length of his room where, removed from the gross and detestable populace, he enjoys his stroll. He pulls the fringes of his literary gown back and forth, kicks out first one foot, then the other, projects his chest in one direction and then in the other, and makes the gesture of throwing to the ground the flea that he holds between his two fingers, and while doing all these things—with the commentary under his arm, with his frowning forehead immersed in thought, his eyebrows turned up and eyes all rounded, with the expression of the man who is wonderstruck —he utters the following dictum, ending it with a markedly emphatic sigh which will carry it to the ears of the surrounding listeners: *Hucusque alii philosophi non pervenerunt* ('No other philosopher has ever reached such a height')."

whose name I happen to recall in this rapid survey. I must limit myself to brief references, and leave for a better occasion a complete study and anthology of the Italian humorists, which would be out of place here due to the specific purpose of the present essay. It will suffice to recall only a few names. We have already mentioned two eminent writers. A third would be a more modest one who came from the people and was a craftsman, accustomed, as he himself said, "to do battle all day with the needle and shears; and although these are tools that are more appropriate for women —the Muses are women—the record, however, nowhere indicates that they were ever used by them."[8] I mean Giambattista Gelli, who nourished himself on philosophy in the Rucellai gardens and who published *Circe* and *I capricci del bottaio,* works which —I repeat—would probably have been considered masterpieces of humor, had they been authored in English by an Englishman.

But seriously, if Congreve, Steele, Prior, and Gay are considered humorists in England, shall we not find, in Italian literature of the eighteenth century, and even of two or three centuries earlier, writers who can be contrasted with them and whom we ourselves never dreamed of calling humorists? And how many quite bizarre and playful minds could we find among the Italian *baioni* (witty jesters) of the sixteenth century! And Cellini? Seriously now, if Pope's *Dunciad* is continually held up before us, don't we have a whole body of literature from which we can draw enough to bury Pope's work and of which we are usually ashamed, starting with Annibal Caro's *I Mattaccini?* As if we did not have the battles of ink fought among Italian writers all through history, from Cecco Angiolieri's sonnets against Dante to Mario Rapisardi's *Atlantide!* Yes, for this too is laughter, to be sure: a bitter kind of joviality, humor, that is to say, bile, or, as Brunetto Latini called it, dry and cold anger, or melancholy in its original sense: the melancholy, precisely, of Swift the libelist. I am thinking of Franco, of Aretino, and—closer to us in time—of the terrifying Monsignor Lodovico Sergardi. Only of them? But there is clearly more than one whom

è forza ch'io riguardi,
il qual mi grida, e di lontano accenna,
e priega ch'io nol lasci nela penna (*O. f.,* XV, 9)

(I must turn my attention to,
who calls to me, and motions from afar,
and begs me not to leave him in my pen),

8 Letter to Don Francesco di Toledo, prefacing Gelli's *La sporta.* [tr.]

because he has seen how generous other critics are in permitting writers to get aboard this *Narrenschiff* of humor. And why not indeed include you, Ortensio Lando, even though you do not choose to act like a madman, as Brutus did, in order to have the right to live and speak freely, as Carlo Tenca said; you too can come aboard, as author of *Paradossi* and of *Commentario delle cose più notabili e mostruose d'Italia e d'altri luoghi,* and if only because you had the courage in your day to call Aristotle a clumsy beast. If it were strictly up to me, I would leave you on land with all the others, like Doni, Boccalini, and Tacitus, the proconsul of the island Lesbos; on land with Dotti; on land with many others who lived before and after you: Caporali, Lippi, and Passeroni. But I don't want to be the only one to be so inflexible, especially since I see that a passenger on the boat and one who unquestionably belongs there, Laurence Sterne, is motioning to Passeroni to come aboard.

What about Alessandro Tassoni? Is he to be left behind too? In the recent celebrations held in his honor, many have claimed to see the makings of a true humorist in this poet whose work shows a sharp and acid scorn, or rather contempt, for his times. If he had been English or German, he would have been a passenger aboard that ship for quite some time now, deserving of such a place "by universal suffrage of the sages" (*Orlando furioso,* XXIV, 1).

We are back where we started: how are we to understand humor? Arcoleo, at the conclusion of his second lecture, declares that he has no inclination for the criticism which, with respect to literary forms, is ready to deal out excommunications and ostracize. He also says that there are complex reasons why humor as a form did not thrive very well in Italy, and that he is unwilling to treat this subject lightly since it deserves a special study. We saw earlier what these complex reasons are, which, in the light of the very examples cited by Arcoleo, often appear to be contradictory: we Italians lack the spirit of observation and intimacy of style, we are pedantic and academic, skeptical and indifferent, and have no aspirations. In countering these accusations, we have mentioned many names, which never even crossed Arcoleo's mind. Only once, when speaking about Heine who, late in life, laughs at his grief, does Arcoleo think, quite by chance, of Leopardi, who also felt that he was like "a tree trunk that suffers and lives," and who wrote to Brighenti: "Here I am ridiculed, spat upon, mistreated by everyone, and it horrifies me just to think about it. And yet *I get myself accustomed to laughing,* which I do successfully."[9] Yes, but "he remained a lyric poet," Arcoleo remarks, "his classical education prevented him from being a humorist." Leopardi, however, also wrote certain dialogues, if we are not mistaken, and certain short prose pieces and essays. When he wrote those, was he also a lyric poet? The classical education . ... But perhaps Manzoni's romantic tendency at least permitted him to be a humorist? Not a chance. His Don Abbondio "aspires to nothing, caught up between duty and fear; he is definitely ridiculous."[10] Isn't this a rather hasty way to judge and reject a writer? But this is literally what Arcoleo does throughout his two lectures: the subject is treated with flashes and final judgments. Humor: a fireworks of exploding definitions; its first phase, doubt and skepticism: *to laugh at one's own thought*—Hamlet; its second phase, struggle and adaptation: *to laugh at one's own suffering*—Don Juan.[11] Among the humorists of the first type he names two Frenchmen, Rabelais and Montaigne, and two Englishmen, Swift and Sterne. Among the humorists of the second type he names two Germans, Richter and Heine, three Englishmen, Carlyle, Dickens, Thackeray, and then . . . Mark Twain. As one can see, not a single Italian, even though the list extends as far as Mark Twain. Arcoleo concludes with this:

Our comic spirit was left enclosed in the embryo of the *Commedia dell'arte* or in dialect poetry; in contrast, irony and satire had a rich and broad development equally in verse and prose, in poems and short stories, in novels and essays. To confuse these forms with humor proper is all one needs to do in order to produce an evaluation opposite to mine or to show that I exaggerate or am unfair. I do not intend to speak about provisional studies or outlines; these are readily found, in all forms of presentation, in any history of art. I however fail to see a humorous literature in Italian, and to support that, I would only need to make a comparison between Ariosto and Cervantes.[12]

We made such a comparison earlier, based on a criterion that does not run counter to Arcoleo's own, if he had carried out the comparison. We should note, however, that Cervantes—like Rabelais and Montaigne—is a Latin; and we don't believe that the Reformation, particularly in Spain . . . But, let's drop the

[9] Quoted in Arcoleo, p. 62. For the exact text see G. Leopardi, *Tutte le opere: Le lettere,* ed. F. Flora (Milan: Mondadori, 1955), 322. [tr.]

[10] Arcoleo, p. 95. [tr.]

[11] *Ibid.,* p. 14. [tr.]

[12] *Ibid.,* p. 93. [tr.]

subject and get back to Italy. We do not wish at all to confuse the comic spirit, irony, or satire with humor: quite to the contrary! Neither should true humor be confused with English humor, that is, with the characteristic mode of laughter or humor which the English, like all other peoples, also have. No one expects the Italians or the French to possess English humor; as no one can expect the English to laugh like the Italians or to use the French *esprit*. They may have even done so occasionally, this doesn't prove anything. True humor is something else; and even for the English it is an *eccentricity of style*. To confuse one thing with the other—we, in our turn, also maintain—is enough to lead the critic to recognize a humoristic literature in one country and to deny its existence in another. And yet a humoristic literature can only be established on this condition, that is, by making this confusion; each people, then, will have its own, which will consist of all the works in which this typical humor is expressed in the most eccentric ways. We can begin our humoristic literature, for example, with Cecco Angiolieri, as the English begin theirs with Chaucer— and I would not say that they begin it well, not because of the poet's worth, but rather because he shows that he mixed into his national drink a bit of the wine harvested in the country of sunlight. Otherwise, a true humoristic literature is not possible among any people: there can only be humorists, that is to say, a few, rare writers who, by natural inclination, will have that complicated and very peculiar psychological process which is called humor. How many such writers does Arcoleo mention?

There is no doubt that humor originates out of a special state of mind, which can, to some degree, spread. When an artistic expression succeeds in dominating the attention of the public, the latter immediately begins to think, speak, and write in accordance with the impressions it has received; thus, such an expression, originating from the particular intuition of a writer, soon penetrates into the public and is then variously transformed and regulated by it. This is what happened with Romanticism and with Naturalism: they became the ideas of their times, almost an ideal atmosphere; and many writers, because of the vogue, acted like romantics or naturalists; in the same manner, many writers acted like humorists in England during the eighteenth century, and many joined the *umidi* in sixteenth century Italy or the *arcadi* in the seventeenth century. A state of mind can be created and become real, or remain imaginary, depending on whether it responds or not to the unique characteristics of our psychic organism. Later, the ideas of a period are transformed, the fashion changes, and the pilot-fishes set out to follow behind other ships. Who will endure? Only a few writers—one can count them on his fingers—the few that originally had the extraordinary intuition, or those in whom that special state of mind became so real that they succeeded in creating an organic work of art capable of resisting time and fashion.

Furthermore, does Arcoleo earnestly believe that there is nothing more than a comic spirit in our literature in dialect? He is a Sicilian, and surely has read Meli, and he knows how unfair is the judgment of *arcadia superiore* given to his poetry, which was sung not only on the shepherd's pipes but also on all the chords of the lyre and with a great variety of forms. Isn't there true humor in a considerable part of Meli's poetry? We would only have to cite La cutuliata to substantiate it:

Tic, tic, finíu . . . Cutuliata.
(Tic, tic, and it's ended . . . Cutuliata.)

And isn't there humor, true humor, in so many of Belli's sonnets? And, not to speak about Maggi's characters, aren't Carlo Porta's *Giovannin Bongee* and *Marchionn di gamb avert* ("Melchior the straddler") two humoristic masterpieces? Since we are speaking about imperishable character types, what about Bersezio's *Monsù Travet* and Gallina's *Il Nobilomo Vidal?*

There is another excellent dialect writer, who is still practically unknown, an indisputably authentic humorist and—it seems as if done purposely—very much a Southerner, from Reggio Calabria. He is Giovanni Merlino, who was brought to the public's attention for the first time a few years ago in a lecture by his compatriot, Giuseppe Mantica.[13] (The latter also would have been a vigorous humorist if politics, in the brief course of his life, had not prematurely distracted him from literature.) Merlino wrote his books for fifty-five readers, whom he names individually; he divides them into four categories, and imposes on each of them special obligations as compensation for the pleasure they derive from his work. One of his volumes, all of which are still unpublished, is entitled *Miscellanea di varie cose sconnesse e piacevoli* ("A miscellany of various things disconnected and pleasant"), "written for those with limited intelligence who want effective

13 Giuseppe Mantica, *Giovanni Merlino* (Naples: Pierro, 1898).

instruction on how to lose it completely." The other volumes bear the title, *Memorie utili et inutili ai posteri, ossia la vita di Giovanni Merlino del quondam Antonino di Reggio, principiata a 27 decembre 1789 e proseguita fino al 1850, composta di sette volumi* ("Useful and useless memories, that is, the life of Giovanni Merlino by the late Antonino di Reggio, begun on December 27, 1789 and continued up to 1850, written in seven volumes"). I wish I could cite at length here the long *Dialogo alla calabrese tra Domine Dio e Giovanni Merlino* ("Dialog in the Calabrese style between our Lord and Giovanni Merlino") or the *Conto con Domine Dio* ("The reckoning with God our Lord") in order to demonstrate what a humorist Merlino was. While we wait for his heirs to release the volumes for publication, I recommend the edition which Mantica made of these two incomparable *Dialoghi* that includes the Italian translation on facing pages.

So much for dialect literature. As for Italian writers, does Arcolco seriously find nothing but irony and satire in their work? I am thinking of a certain *Socrate immaginario* written by a certain eighteenth century abbot; and I am thinking of Foscolo's *Didimo Chierico; of* some of Baretti's flights in prose; I am thinking of Manzoni's *I promessi sposi,* which is completely permeated with genuine humor,[14] and of Giusti's *Sant'Ambrogio,* a truly humorous poem, perhaps the only truly humorous among all his satirical and sentimental poems; I am thinking of certain dialogues and prose writings by Leopardi; I am thinking of Guerrazzi's *L'asino* ("The donkey") and *Il buco nel muro* ("The hole in the wall"), and of D'Azeglio's *Fanfulla;* I am thinking of Carlo Bini; I am thinking of that certain kitchen in the Fratti castle in Nievo's *Confessioni d'un ottuagenario* ("Confessions of an eighty year old"); I am thinking of Camillo De Meis, of Revere; and since Arcoleo comes up as far as Mark Twain, I am thinking of Cantoni's *Un re umorista, Il demonio dello stile, L'altalena delle antipatie, Pietro e Paola, Scaricalasino, L'Illustrissimo* ("A king humorist," "The demon of style," "The swing of dislikes," "Peter and Paula," "Unload-the-donkey," "Most illustrious"); of De Marchi's *Demetrio Pianelli;* I am thinking of the poets of the *scapigliatura lombarda* ("the Lombardian bohemianism") and of so many passages of pure and profound humor in Carducci's and Graf's poetry; I am thinking of the numerous humoristic char-

---

[14] See Part II for my analysis of the humor of Don Abbondio, who seems to Arcoleo to be definitely a ridiculous or comic figure.

acters who fill the novels and short stories of Fogazzaro, Farina, Capuana, Fucini, and also of some of the works by younger writers from Luigi Antonio Villari to Albertazzi, to Panzini . . . And while we have the last named writer in mind, I would like to put his *Lanterna di Diogene* in Arcoleo's left hand and the candle of Bruno's *Candelaio* in his right hand; I am certain that he would discover many humorists in medieval and modern Italian literature.

PART TWO

THE ESSENCE, CHARACTERISTICS, AND SUBSTANCE OF HUMOR

I

What is humor? If we should take into account all the answers that have been given to this question, all the definitions attempted by writers and critics, we could fill many pages and probably at that point, confused by so many differing opinions, we could do nothing more than to repeat the question: But what, in short, is humor?

We mentioned earlier that all those who have taken up the subject, either by design or by accident, are in agreement about one thing only, that humor is truly very difficult to define because it has infinite varieties and so many characteristics that any attempt at a general definition would risk forgetting some of them.

This is true; but it is also true that for some time now we should have realized that to start from these characteristics is not the best way to arrive at an understanding of the true essence of humor, for it always happens that the characteristic that is taken as fundamental is the one that is found to be common to several works or to several writers studied with special interest. The result is that there are as many definitions of humor as characteristics that have been found, and all of them naturally have an element of truth, and yet none is the true definition.

To be sure, from the sum total of all these various characteristics and resultant definitions, one can arrive at some understanding, in general terms, of what humor is; but it will always be a summary and external view, precisely because it is based on summary and external factors.

Some characteristics are not found in all humorists. Among them are, for instance: the characteristic of that peculiar kindliness or benevolent indulgence some perceive in humor, which was once defined by Richter as "the melancholy of a superior mind which goes so far as to amuse itself with the very thing that causes it to be sad"; and, to quote from Sully's *An Essay on Laughter,* that "quiet survey of things, at once playful and reflective," that "mode of greeting amusing shows which seems, in its moderation, to be both an indulgence in the sense of fun and an expiation for the rudeness of such indulgence," and that certain "outward expansive movement of the spirits met and retarded by a cross-current of something like kindly thoughtfulness."[1] Some of these traits—which Sully, among others, regards as principal in humor—can be found in some writers and not in others; actually some writers may show traits that are opposite to them, as in the case of Swift who is melancholy in the original meaning of the word, that is, full of bile. In any case, we shall see later, when we speak of Manzoni's Don Abbondio, what after all that peculiar kindliness or thoughtful benevolence really consists of.

On the contrary, Bonghi's definition of humor as a "sour disposition to disclose and express the ridiculous aspect of seriousness and the serious aspect of the ridiculous" will apply to Swift and to those humorists who, like him, are sardonic and mordant, but it will not apply to other writers. Furthermore, this manner of understanding humor is not complete, as Lipps himself has remarked against Lazarus' theory which also holds humor to be a disposition of the spirit; nor is Hegel's understanding complete when he says that humor is "a special attitude of the intellect and of the spirit which enables the artist to project himself into the

---

[1] One can quote many definitions by Richter. Among other things, he calls humor "the sublime inverted," but the best description of his own way of understanding humor is the one we mentioned earlier, when we spoke about the difference between the comic sense of the ancients and that of the moderns: "Romantic humor is the serious attitude of the person who compares the small finite world with the infinite idea: from that, a philosophical laughter results which is a mixture of pain and grandeur. This sense of the comic is universal, that is, full of tolerance and sympathy for all those who, sharing in our nature, etc." Elsewhere [*Vorschule der Aesthetik,* VII–VIII] he speaks of that "idea which annihilates," which has had a great deal of success with the German critics, although it was applied by them in a less philosophical sense. Lipps says: "Humor can finally be fully conscious. It is also like that when the protagonist himself is conscious not only of the right but also the rightfulness of his own point of view, not only of his sublimity but also of his relative nothingness" (*Komik und Humor,* p. 238). For the quotations from James Sully, see his *An Essay on Laughter* (London, 1902), p. 299, Fr. tr., *Essai sur le rire* (Paris: Alcan, 1904).

place of things," a definition that has the earmarks of a riddle, if one does not assume Hegel's own point of view.[2]

Other characteristics, more common and therefore more generally observed, are: a fundamental "contradiction" which is usually said to derive principally from the discord which feeling and meditation discover either between real life and the human ideal or between human aspirations and human frailty and miseries, and whose main effect is a certain perplexity between weeping and laughing; the skepticism which gives color to all humorous observations and descriptions; and, finally, the minutely and even cunningly analytical process of that skepticism.

From all these characteristics and resultant definitions, I repeat, one can reach an understanding, in general terms, of what humor is, but it will undeniably be an understanding which is too summary. For if, besides a few determining factors that are totally incomplete, as we have seen, there are others that are unquestionably more common, the inner reason of the latter is not seen at all distinctly nor explained.

Shall we renounce seeing it clearly and explaining it, and thereby accept the opinion of Benedetto Croce who declared that humor, like all psychological states, is undefinable, and who, in his *Estetica,* counted it among the many esthetic concepts of the sympathetic? Croce says:

Philosophers have long labored in examining these facts, especially those like the *comic,* which heads the list, the *sublime,* the *tragic,* the *humorous,* and the *amusing.* Yet we should avoid the error of considering them *special emotions,* as *signs* of the emotions, which leads to accepting distinctions and classes of emotions, whereas organic emotion in itself cannot give rise to classes; and we need to clarify in what sense they can be called *mixed* facts. The latter give rise to *complex* concepts, that is, to complexes of facts in which pleasant or unpleasant organic emotions (or spiritual-organic emotions) play a part, as do certain external circumstances which supply a definable content to those merely organic or spiritual-organic emotions. The method of defining these concepts is the *genetic*: placing the organism in situation *A,* when circumstance *B* arises, the result is fact *C.*

These and other similar processes have no contact with the esthetic fact beyond the general contact that all of them, insofar as they constitute the stuff of reality, can become the object of artistic representation, and beyond the accidental relation which occurs when esthetic facts occa-

[2] Bonghi, *op. cit.* in Chap. II; Lipps, *op. cit.;* Hegel, *Aesthetiks,* Vol. I, Pt. II, Section III, Chap. III. [tr.]

sionally enter these processes, as in the case of the impression of the sublime inspired by the work of a Titanic artist, such as Dante or Shakespeare, and of the comic produced by the attempts of a dauber or scribbler. But in these cases too the process is external to the esthetic fact, for the only feelings linked to the esthetic fact are the feelings of pleasure and displeasure, of the esthetic value and disvalue, of the beautiful and the ugly.[3]

In the first place, why are psychological states undefinable? They may be undefinable to a philosopher, but the artist, in essence, does nothing else but define and give artistic representation to psychological states. Furthermore, if humor is a process or a fact which gives rise to complex concepts, that is, to complexes of facts, how does it then become itself a concept? A concept will be what originates from humor, not humor itself. Surely, if we take the esthetic fact to be what Croce understands it to be, then not only this process but everything else as well will be outside the esthetic fact. But I have shown in the course of this essay and elsewhere that the esthetic fact is not, and cannot be, what Croce understands it to be. Moreover, what is the meaning of the concession that "this and other similar processes have no contact with the esthetic fact beyond the general contact that all of them, insofar as they constitute the stuff of reality, can become the object of artistic *representation*"? Art can represent the process which gives rise to the concept of humor. Now, how can I, as a critic, come to an understanding of this artistic representation, if I do not understand the process that produces it? And what then would esthetic criticism consist of? In his essay on esthetic criticism Cesareo remarks:

If a work of art is to produce a state of mind, it seems evident that the more intense and harmonious the various contributing elements are, the more complete the final effect will be. Also in esthetics the sum total is the result of the individual terms. The analysis of each particular expression, one by one, will give the measure of the general expression. *Now since the perfect reproduction of a state of mind, which is just what esthetic beauty consists of, is an emotional fact which can only result from the sum total of a number of feelings represented, then the psychological analysis of a work of art is the necessary foundation of any esthetic evaluation.*[4]

[3] Benedetto Croce, *Estetica* (Milan, Palermo, Naples: Remo Sandron, 1902), pp. 90–91, 92–93. For the statement on humor as undefinable, see Croce's "L'umorismo: Del vario significato della parola e dell'uso nella critica letteraria," *Journal of Comparative Literature*, I (1903), 220–228.

[4] G. A. Cesareo, "La critica estetica," *Critica militante* (Messina: Trimarchi, 1907), p. 11. [tr.]

Speaking about the present essay, in connection with Baldensperger's study, "Les définitions de l'humour," Croce is pleased to say that Baldensperger mentions also the studies made by Cazamian, a Bergsonian, who argues that humor eludes scientific inquiry because its typical and constant elements are few in number and are, above all, negative, whereas its variable elements are countless.[5] As a result, the task for criticism is to study the content and tone of each example of humor, that is, the personality of each humorist. According to Mr. Baldensperger, *there is no such thing as humor, there are only humorists.* And Croce hastens to conclude that "the question is thus exhausted."

Exhausted? But we ask and shall ask again and again how it is that, if humor does not exist and cannot be defined, there are writers who can be identified and defined as humorists. On what basis can they be recognized and identified as such? There is no *humor,* there are only humorists; the *comic* does not exist, there are only comic writers. Fine! And if someone mistakes a certain humorist for a comic writer, how can I show him that he is mistaken and that the author in question is indeed a humorist and not a comic writer?

Croce postulates a procedural obstacle regarding the possibility of defining a concept. I, in turn, put a specific case to him and raise the question of how could he prove to Arcoleo, for instance, that Don Abbondio is not a comic character, as he asserts, but a humoristic character, if he did not have a clear idea in his mind of what humor is and of how it should be understood. But then Croce says that, after all, he is not really attacking the definitions, and that he can reject all of them, on the philosophical level, by way of accepting them on the empirical level. This acceptance includes also my definition of humor, which moreover is not, nor was it meant to be, a definition, but is rather an explanation of the inner process which takes place, and must inevitably take place, in all the writers called humorists.

Croce's esthetics is so abstract and negative that to apply it to literary criticism is absolutely impossible unless it is repeatedly to reject it, as he himself does when he accepts those so-called

---

[5] Croce, *La Critica,* VII (1909), 219–23. For the Baldensperger reference, see his "Les définitions de l'humour," *Etudes d'historie littéraire* (Paris: Hachette, 1907), pp. 176–222. The article by L. Cazamian, "Pourquoi nous ne pouvons définir l'humour" is in *Revue germanique,* II (1906), 601–634.

empirical concepts which, having been chased out of the door, come back on him through the window.

Oh, how beautifully satisfying philosophy can be!

II

Let us see, then, without further digression, what is the process that results in the particular representation which is customarily called humor; let us see if this representation has its own distinctive traits, and what is their origin, and if there exists a special way of looking at the world which constitutes precisely the substance and explanation of humor.

Ordinarily, as I have written elsewhere[6] and must necessarily repeat now, the work of art is created by the free movement of inner life which organizes the ideas and images into a harmonious form, in which all the elements correspond with one another and with the generating idea that coordinates them. Reflection does not remain inactive, of course, during the conception and during the execution of the work of art: it is present at the birth and throughout the development of the work, follows its progressive phases and derives pleasure from it, and brings all the various elements together, coordinating and comparing them. Consciousness does not illuminate the whole realm of the spirit; particularly in a creative artist consciousness is not an inner light distinct from thought, which might allow the will to draw from it images and ideas as if from a rich source. Consciousness, in short, is not a creative power, but an inner mirror in which thought contemplates itself. One could say rather that consciousness is thought which sees itself watching over what it does spontaneously. As a rule, in the moment of artistic conception, reflection is hidden and remains, as it were, invisible: in the artist, reflection is almost a form of feeling. While the work is slowly taking shape, reflection criticizes it, not coldly and without feeling, as an impartial judge would do in analyzing it, but suddenly, thanks to the impression that it receives from the work.

This is what happens as a rule. Let us see now whether—as a result of the natural temperament of those writers called humorists and as a result of their peculiar way of intuiting and considering man and life—this same process occurs in the conception of the

---

[6] See "Un critico fantastico," which I cited earlier, in my volume *Arte e scienza.*

work of humor; that is, let us see whether reflection plays in it the role just described or whether it acquires a special function.

Now, we shall see that during the conception of all works of humor, reflection is not hidden, it does not remain invisible: it is not, that is, almost a form of feeling or almost a mirror in which feeling contemplates itself; rather, it places itself squarely before the feeling, in a judging attitude, and, detaching itself from it, analyzes it and disassembles its imagery; from this analysis and decomposition, however, there arises or emerges a new feeling which could be called and in fact I call the *feeling of the opposite.*

I see an old lady whose hair is dyed and completely smeared with some kind of horrible ointment; she is all made-up in a clumsy and awkward fashion and is all dolled-up like a young girl. I begin to laugh. I *perceive* that she is *the opposite* of what a respectable old lady should be. Now I could stop here at this initial and superficial comic reaction: the comic consists precisely of this *perception of the opposite.* But if, at this point, reflection interferes in me to suggest that perhaps this old lady finds no pleasure in dressing up like an exotic parrot, and that perhaps she is distressed by it and does it only because she pitifully deceives herself into believing that, by making herself up like that and by concealing her wrinkles and gray hair, she may be able to hold the love of her much younger husband—if reflection comes to suggest all this, then I can no longer laugh at her as I did at first, exactly because the inner working of reflection has made me go beyond, or rather enter deeper into, the initial stage of awareness: from the beginning *perception of the opposite,* reflection has made me shift to a *feeling of the opposite.* And herein lies the precise difference between the comic and humor.

Another illustration: "Oh sir, my dear sir! Perhaps all this seems *ludicrous* to you as it does to others; perhaps I am only burdening you with the stupid and trivial details of my domestic life, but it is not a laughing matter to me, because I feel it all . . ."[7] This is what Marmeladoff cries out to Raskolnikoff in the tavern amid the laughter of the drunken customers. This outcry is precisely the painful and exasperated protest of a humoristic character against someone who, right there before him, dwells on an initial superficial perception of his situation and only succeeds in seeing its comic side.

[7] Dostoevski, *Crime and Punishment,* I, Chap. I. [tr.]

Here is now a third example, which can be taken as typical because it is so clearly explicit. One day Giuseppe Giusti, an Italian poet, enters the church of Sant'Ambrogio in Milan and finds it full of soldiers,

di que' soldati settentrionali,
come sarebbero boemi e croati,
messi qui nella vigna a far da pali

(of those northern soldiers,
as would be Bohemians and Croats,
stuck here in the vineyard to serve as stakes).

His first reaction is a feeling of resentment: those unbending and tough soldiers are there to remind him of his enslaved homeland. But just at that moment the temple resounds with organ music, and then follows a very slow German hymn, sung by the soldiers "d'un suono grave, flebile, solenne" ("in a grave, plaintive and solemn tone"), which is a prayer and sounds like a lament. This music suddenly evokes, in a poet who is accustomed to use the scourge of political and social satire, an unusual mood, a mood which is typical of humor. In other words, it prepares him for that special reflection which, freeing itself from the original emotion of hate provoked by the sight of the soldiers, produces in fact the feeling of the opposite. The poet perceives in the hymn

                la dolcezza amara
dei canti uditi da fanciullo: il core,
che da voce domestica gl'impara,
ce li ripete i giorni del dolore:
un pensier mesto della madre cara,
un desiderio di pace e d'amore,
uno sgomento di lontano esilio . . .

                    (the bitter sweetness
of songs heard in my childhood: the heart,
which learns them from a familiar voice,
repeats them to us in days of sorrow:
a sad thought of our dear mother,
a desire for peace and love,
the dismay of a distant exile).

This makes him think that those soldiers, snatched from their homes by a fearful king,

a dura vita, a dura disciplina,
muti, derisi, solitari stanno,
strumenti ciechi dell'occhiuta rapina,
che lor non tocca e che forse non sanno

(subject to a hard life, to a hard discipline,
they stand silent, mocked, and alone,
blind instruments of sharp-eyed plunder,
which they do not share and of which they may know nothing).

Then the original hate turns into the opposite feeling, and Giusti
sees the soldiers as

povera gente! lontana da' suoi,
in un paese, qui, che le vuol male

(poor people! far from their families,
in a country, here, that hates them).

Finally the poet has to leave the church for

qui, se non fuggo, abbraccio un caporale,
colla su' brava mazza di nocciuolo,
duro e piantato lí come un piuolo

(now, if I do not flee, I will embrace a corporal,
with his nice hazel staff,
tough and steady like a picket.)

In noticing this, that is, in perceiving this sense of the opposite
which is produced by a special activity of reflection, I am not at
all leaving the field of esthetic and psychological criticism. The
psychological analysis of this poem is the necessary foundation for
the esthetic evaluation of it. I cannot grasp its beauty unless I
understand the psychological process which results in the exact
reproduction of the state of mind which the poet intended to
evoke, and it is this very reproduction that constitutes esthetic
beauty.

Let us consider now a more complex example, one in which the
special activity of reflection does not make itself readily evident.
Let us take up again a book about which we have already spoken:
Cervantes' *Don Quijote*. We intend to judge its esthetic value.
What shall we do? After reading the text and reacting to it, we will
have to take into account also here the state of mind that the
author set out to awaken in us. What is this state of mind? We
have the urge to laugh at all that is comic in the artistic char-
acterization of this poor deranged man who involves himself and
everybody and everything in the disguise of his madness; we feel
like laughing but the laughter that comes to our lips is not natural
and easy; we sense that something troubles and hampers it, and
this something is a feeling of pity, of sorrow, and even, indeed, of
admiration, because, if the heroic adventures of this poor *hidalgo*

are ludicrous, there is no doubt that he is, in his very ludicrousness, truly heroic. We are dealing with a comic representation, but from it we derive a feeling which either prevents us from laughing or troubles our laughter and makes it bitter. Through the comic itself, we have here also the feeling of the opposite. The author awakens it in us because he experienced it first, for the reasons that we have already mentioned. Now, why is it that in this case the special activity of reflection does not make itself perceptible? Simply because reflection—as a product of the utterly sad experience of his life, an experience which had determined the writer's humoristic disposition—had already exerted itself upon his feelings, upon those feelings that had armed him a religious knight at Lepanto. Freeing itself of those feelings and standing before them in judgment, in a dark jailhouse of La Mancha, and analyzing them with bitter detachment, reflection had already aroused the sense of the opposite in the writer, the result of which was precisely *Don Quijote.* This work is in fact the objectified feeling of the opposite. Unlike Giusti, the author has not given artistic representation to the cause of this process, only to its effect. Consequently, the sense of the opposite is felt through the comic quality of the representation itself: this comic quality is the product of the feeling of the opposite which is evoked in the poet by the special working of reflection upon his original feelings which remain hidden.

Now what need do I have of assigning a particular ethical value to the feeling of the opposite as does Theodor Lipps in his essay *Komik und Humor*? What I am saying—let there be no misunderstanding—is that this sense of the opposite never really occurs to Lipps. On the one hand, he sees both the comic and humor as nothing more than a kind of mechanism, the same mechanism that Croce cites as an example of an acceptable explanation for such "concepts": "placing the organism in situation *A,* when circumstance *B* arises, the result is fact *C.*" On the other hand, Lipps is constantly entangled in ethical values, since for him all artistic and esthetic enjoyment in general is enjoyment of something having an ethical value which is not an element of a complex but rather the object of esthetic intuition. He constantly refers to the ethical value of the human personality, and speaks of a "positive human element" and of the negation of it:

As we have seen, the most comprehensive characteristic of the tragic consists in the fact that by negating that which is positive in man, this positive human element is brought closer to us and its value is perceived more clearly. This is also the essence of humor, except that in humor the negation is of a different kind, namely, it is a comic negation. Speaking of the naive type of the comic, I said that it lies on the line that leads from the comic to humor. This does not mean that the naive comic is the same as humor; rather, even here the comic as such is the opposite of humor. The naive comic arises when that which is justified, good and wise from the viewpoint of the naive temperament, will instead appear in a contrasting light when considered from our viewpoint. Humor, on the contrary, originates when that which in relatively justified, good and wise re-emerges out of the process of comic annihilation and now more than ever becomes evident and is appreciated in its value . . .

The true basis and essence of humor is everywhere and always the relative goodness, beauty, and reason which can be found even where, according to our usual notions, they appear not to exist, indeed to be deliberately denied . . .

In the comic not only the comic itself dissolves into nothing but we ourselves dissolve into nothing in a certain way, with our hopes, our faith in something sublime or grand, and with the rules and habits of our thought, etc. Humor rises above this process of self-annihilation. This humor, the humor we show in the face of the comic, consists ultimately, like the one shown by the agent of the conscious humoristic manifestation, in the freedom of the spirit, in the assurance of our selves and in the certainty that something reasonable, good and sublime exists in the world, and that this something continues to exist in spite of all objective or subjective nothingness, or even becomes apparent by just that.[8]

But Lipps himself is then forced to recognize that "not every humor reaches such a high stage," and that "beside the conciliatory, there is a humor which is torn and divisive."[9]

But to repeat, what need do I have of ascribing some ethical value to what I have called the sense of the opposite or of defining it *a priori* in some way? It will define itself, in each separate instance, according to the writer's personality or the object of the artistic representation. Why should I, as a critic interested in esthetic valuation, concern myself with knowing in whom or where relative reason, and the just and the good, reside? I do not want to leave, nor should I leave, the realm of pure fantasy. I take up any artistic representation, and I propose only to judge its esthetic value. In order to make this judgment, I need first of all to know the state of mind that the work purports to arouse—this I will know from the impression I have received of it. This state of mind,

8 Lipps, p. 234, 237, 240. [tr.]
9 *Ibid.*, p. 240. [tr.]

in each case that I deal with a genuine work of humor, is one of perplexity: I feel as if I were suspended between two forces: I feel like laughing, and I do laugh, but my laughter is troubled and obstructed by something that stems from the representation itself. I look for the cause. In order to find it, I do not have to dissolve at all the work of imagination into an ethical relationship, nor to bring into play the ethical value of the human personality and so on.

I constantly find this feeling of the opposite, whatever it may be, emanating in many ways from the artistic representation itself, in all the works I am accustomed to calling humoristic. Why limit its cause ethically or abstractly by attributing it, for instance, to the conflict which feeling and meditation discover between real life and the human ideal, or between human aspirations and human weaknesses and misery? It may spring also from this, just as from many other sources that cannot be determined *a priori*. Our only concern is to verify that this feeling of the opposite does arise, and that it arises from a special activity which reflection acquires in the conception of such works of art.

III

Let us hold to this; let us pursue this special activity of reflection, and let us see if it does not explain one by one the various characteristics which can be found in all works of humor.

We said that, as a rule, in the conception of a work of art, reflection is almost a form of feeling, almost a mirror in which feeling looks at itself. In pursuing this image, one could say that, in the conception of a work of humor, reflection is indeed like a mirror, but a mirror of icy water, in which the flame of feeling not only looks at itself but also plunges in it and extinguishes itself: the sizzling of the water is the laughter that the humorist evokes; the vapor which it emits is the fantasy, often somewhat murky, of the work of humor.

"There must be justice in this world after all!" exclaims Renzo, the betrothed, stirred by passion and rebellion. "The truth is that a man overcome by grief has no longer any notion of what he is saying," observes Manzoni.[10] The former is the flame of feeling; the latter is that flame as it is submerged and extinguished in the icy water of reflection.

10 Manzoni, *I promessi sposi*, Chap. III. [tr.]

Reflection, engaging in its special activity, comes to disturb and to interrupt the spontaneous movement that organizes ideas and images into a harmonious form. It has often been observed that humoristic works are disorganized, disconnected, interrupted by constant digressions. Even in a work as harmonious in its total design as *I promessi sposi*, critics have noticed an occasional defect of composition, the excessive detail in some passages, and the frequent interruptions in the narrative that are caused either by references to the famous "anonymous" or by the witty intrusions of the author himself. These things, which for Italian critics are in one way an excess and in another way a defect, constitute the most obvious characteristic of all humoristic books. It is enough to mention Sterne's *Tristram Shandy*, which from beginning to end is a tangle of divergencies and digressions, in spite of the autobiographer's intention to narrate everything *ab ovo*, point by point, beginning with his mother's womb and with the clock that Mr. Shandy, Senior, was in the habit of winding punctually.

But if this characteristic has received attention, its underlying causes have yet to be clearly seen. The disorganization, the digressions and divergencies do not derive from the writer's eccentricities or personal whim, but are precisely the necessary and inevitable consequence of the disturbance and disruption which are produced in the organizing movement of the images through the work of the active reflection, which evokes an association through contraries: in other words, the images, instead of being linked through similarity or juxtaposition, are presented in conflict: each image, each group of images evokes and attracts contrary ones, and these naturally divide the spirit which, in its restlessness, is obstinately determined to find or establish the most astonishing relationships between these images.

Every genuine humorist is not only a poet, he is a critic as well, but—let us take note—a critic *sui generis*, a fantastical critic: I say "fantastical" not only in the sense of bizarre or whimsical, but also in its esthetic sense, although at first glance the two meanings may seem to be contradictory.[11] But that's really how it is, and this is why I have always spoken of a *special* activity of reflection.

This will become clear when one realizes that, even though the

---

[11] By "fantastical" in the esthetic sense Pirandello implies that the humorist is a critic that is capable of employing his fantasy in his work, rather than a critic who relies solely on his reason and judgment; cf. Pirandello's essay "Un critico fantastico," cited earlier. [tr.]

peculiar temperament known as humoristic can unquestionably be determined by an innate or inherited melancholy, the sad vicissitudes or a bitter experience of life, or also by a pessimistic or skeptical outlook as a result of study and of meditation on human existence and on the destiny of man, etc., that temperament, by itself, is not enough to create a work of art. The humoristic disposition is nothing but the soil made ready: the work of art is the seed that will fall into that soil, will sprout, and will develop by nurturing itself on the soil's humor, that is to say, drawing upon its condition and quality. But the birth and growth of this plant must be spontaneous. That is why the seed falls only into soil prepared to receive it, that is, where it can best germinate. The creation of art is spontaneous; it is not an external composition, the adding of elements whose relationships have been studied: a living organism cannot be composed by grafting and combining separate members. A work of art, in short, is a work of art to the degree that it is *ingenuous,* it cannot be the result of conscious reflection.

Therefore, the reflection of which I speak is not in opposition to the conscious versus the spontaneous; it is a kind of projection of the very activity of the creating imagination: it originates from the mental image like the shadow from a body; it has all the characteristics of *ingenuousness* or of spontaneous birth; it is in the seed itself of creation, and that which I have called the feeling of the opposite emanates, in fact, from it.

This is why I added that humor could be considered a phenomenon of doubling in the act of artistic conception. The conception of the work of art is essentially nothing more than a form of the organization of images. The artist's idea is not an abstract one; it is a feeling which becomes the hub of internal life, takes possession of the spirit, stirs it, and by stirring it, tends to create for itself a body of images. As a rule, when an emotion excites the spirit, all the ideas and all the images that are in harmony with that emotion are likewise aroused; in the case of humor, instead, because reflection is inserted into the seed of the emotion like a malignant viscous growth, only ideas and images conflicting with the emotion are aroused. This is the condition and the quality that the seed acquires, as I mentioned earlier, when it falls into the soil: the viscous germ of reflection penetrates the seed; the plant sprouts and is dressed in a green which is foreign and yet is innately its own.

At this point Croce steps forward with the whole force of his logic, condensed to a "thus," to infer from my position as stated above that I hold art and humor to be in opposition. Then he asks:

Does Pirandello mean to say that humor is not art or that it is more than art? And in this case, what really is it? Reflection on art, and thus criticism of art? Reflection on life, and thus a philosophy of life? Or is it a unique form of the spirit whose existence philosophers have not hitherto known about? If Pirandello himself has discovered it, by all means he should have demonstrated what it is, assigned it a place, and established the differences and relationships that it has with other forms of the spirit. Instead of doing this, he merely states that humor is the opposite of art.[12]

I find myself thoroughly confused. But where, but when have I ever made such a statement? It comes to one of two things: either I do not know how to write or Croce does not know how to read. What does reflection *on* art (which is criticism of art) and reflection *on* life (which is philosophy of life) have to do with what I said? I said that, *as a rule,* generally speaking, in the conception of a work of art, that is, while a writer is conceiving it, reflection has a role which I have sought to define as a first step toward determining what special activity reflection exercises not *on* the work of art, but rather *in* that *special* work of art that we call humoristic. Now, does this make humor non-art or more than art? Who says so? Croce himself says it because he wants to say it, not because I did not express myself clearly when I showed that humor is art with a characteristic of its own and when I clarified that its source is a special activity of reflection, which decomposes the image created by an original feeling in order that from this decomposition a contrary emotion may arise and be present, precisely as we have seen from the examples cited, and from all the other examples that I could have cited through a detailed analysis of each of the most famous works of humor.

I should not like to accept as valid the hypothesis, which is quite offensive to Croce, that he believes that a work of art is concocted like ordinary pastry, with so many eggs, so much flour, so much of this or that ingredient which may or may not be used. But unfortunately he forces me to accept such a hypothesis when, in order to give me "a tangible proof that humor as art cannot be dis-

---

[12] Croce, *op. cit.* in note 5 above. [tr.]

tinguished from the totality of art," he presents two cases concerning reflection, which—according to him—I intend to assume as the
distinctive characteristic of the art of humor, as though referring
to reflection in general were the same as speaking, as I do, of a
special activty of reflection, understood more as an inner process
which is never lacking in the act of conception and creation of such
works than as a distinctive characteristic which must inevitably
manifest itself. But let's avoid going into that. Croce presents, I
was saying, these two cases: reflection "either enters as a component
in the substance of the work of art, and in this case, there is no
difference of any kind between humor and comedy (or tragedy, or
lyrical poetry, etc.) since thought and reflection enter or may enter
all works of art; or it remains external to the work of art, and then
we have criticism and not art, not even humoristic art."[13]

There it is, the usual mixture. The *recipe:* so much fantasy, so
much emotion, so much reflection; mix and you will have a work
of art, because all those ingredients, and even others, can be introduced into the *composition* of a work of art.

But may I ask: what has this mixture, this *composition* of elements as *matter* of the work of art, whatever and however it may
be, got to do with that which I have said and clarified, point by
point, by commenting, for example, on Giusti's *Sant'Ambrogio,*
where I demonstrated how reflection, inserting itself like a viscous
growth into the poet's original emotion, which consists of hate
towards foreign soldiers, converts, by gradual process, that original
emotion into its opposite? And since this reflection, which is always
on guard and continually mirror-like during artistic creation, does
not accompany the original emotion in this instance but at a
certain point opposes it—does it perhaps for that reason become
extrinsic to the work of art, does it for that reason become criticism? I am talking about an intrinsic *activity* of reflection, and
not about reflection as *material component* of the work of art. It
is quite clear! And it is difficult to believe that Croce does not
understand that. He doesn't want to. The proof of it is his attempt
to show that my distinctions are vague, and that I constantly repeat, modify, and attenuate them, and that I resort to imagery
when I don't know what else to say. Instead, I challenge anyone to
find, in the examples Croce gives of my alleged repetitions, modifications, and providential recourse to images, the slightest incon-

[13] *Ibid.* [tr.]

sistency, the slightest modification, the slightest attenuation of my original premise, rather than a clearer explanation or a more precise image; I challenge anyone to recognize, as Croce does, my embarrassment in that my concepts, as he puts it, dissolve in my hands when I take them up to present them to others.

This is all so pitiful. But such is the hold on Croce of a statement he once let slip, namely, that it is neither warranted nor possible to speak of humor.

Let us proceed.

IV

In order for us to understand the reason for the contrast between reflection and emotion, we must penetrate the ground on which the seed falls, that is to say, the humorist's spirit. If it is true that the humoristic disposition by itself is not sufficient, since it needs the seed of creation, this seed then nurtures itself on the humor that it finds. Lipps himself—who distinguishes three categories of humor: a) humor as disposition, or way of seeing things, b) humor as representation, and c) objective humor—comes then to the conclusion that actually humor exists only in the writer that has it: subjectivism and objectivism are nothing more than different attitudes of the spirit in the act of representation. In other words, the representation of humor, which always exists in the writer who has it, can have either a subjective or an objective attitude.

Those three categories present themselves to Lipps because he limits and determines ethically the cause of humor, which is for him, as we saw earlier, the sublimation of the comic by means of the comic itself. We know what he means by sublimation. I have humor, according to him, when "I am the one who feels superior, the one who affirms himself, the agent of wisdom and morality. Then I view the world from the point of view of my perfection or in the light of that perfection. I find funny things in the world and I engage in thoughts about the comic. But finally I reaffirm myself from within, as my sense of superiority is elevated, strengthened and exalted."[14]

Now in our opinion this notion is, in the first place, absolutely alien to humor, and furthermore it is one-sided. If we remove the

[14] Lipps, p. 242. [tr.]

ethical value from the formula, what remains then may be taken, at best, as humor viewed with respect to its effect, not its cause.

My view is that the comic and its opposite are both present in the humoristic disposition itself and are inherent in the process which results from it. The condition of a man who is constantly somewhat off key, who is like a violin and double bass at the same time; of a man in which a thought cannot originate without the opposite or contrary thought originating at the same time, and who finds that for each reason he has to say *yes,* there arise one or more that compel him to say *no* and keep him suspended in perplexity for the rest of his life; of a man who cannot give into a feeling without suddenly perceiving something inside him which mocks, disturbs, disconcerts and taunts him—is a condition which, in its very abnormality, can only be bitterly comic.

This same contrast, which is in the temperament of the humorist, can be perceived in reality and then enters the artistic representation. It is a special form of the mind, to which it is totally arbitrary to attribute a determining cause. It may be due to a bitter experience of life and of human relationships, of an experience which, while on the one hand, no longer, permitting the spontaneous feeling to take wing and to rise like a nightingale to sing in the sunlight without catching it and holding it back by the tail as it begins its upward flight, leads us, on the other hand, to reflect that the evil nature of man is often due to the misery of life and to the misfortunes which abound in life and which not all people know how or are able to bear. It leads us to reflect that since life is fatally lacking in what from the point of view of human reason would be a clear and definite purpose, it becomes necessary for life, if it is not to drift aimlessly in the void, to have a particular, fictitious and illusory purpose for each human being, whether of low or high station. Since this is not, nor can it ever be, the true purpose of life, it matters little that everyone desperately seeks it and no one finds it, perhaps because it does not exist; what matters is that we give importance to something, however fictitious: it will be worth as much as something thought to be real, since in the final analysis neither one nor the other will bring any satisfaction: so much so that man's thirst for knowledge will continue forever unabated, his constant longing will never be extinguished, and unfortunately it cannot be said that man's happiness consists in progress.

We shall see that all fictions of the spirit, all the creations of feeling are the basic material of humor; that is, we shall see that reflection becomes something resembling a diabolical imp that takes apart the mechanism of each image, of each phantasm produced by the emotions; it takes it apart in order to see how it is made; it releases the mainspring, and the whole mechanism squeaks convulsively. It may happen that this is done sometimes with that "kind indulgence" which is mentioned by those who conceive only of a good-natured humor. But we should not rely on that, because if the humorist's temperament sometimes has that characteristic, that is to say, that indulgence, sympathy, or even pity, we should recall that they are the result of reflection which has acted upon the opposite feeling; they are a feeling of the opposite arising from reflection upon those events, emotions, and people that at the same time arouse indignation, spite, and mockery in the humorist, who is as sincere in the latter feelings as he is in his indulgence, sympathy, or pity. If this were not true, we would not have authentic humor but rather irony, which derives—as we saw— from a contradiction that is merely verbal, from a rhetorical dissimulation that is absolutely contrary to the nature of genuine humor.

Every feeling, every thought, or every impulse that arises in the humorist immediately splits into its contrary: every affirmative into a negative, which finally ends up assuming the same value as the affirmative. At times perhaps, the humorist can pretend to have only one feeling; meanwhile, inside him, the other feeling speaks to him, a feeling that at first seems to lack the courage to expose itself; it speaks to him and it begins to advance now a timid excuse, now an attenuation, which reduce the warmth of the original feeling, now an acute reflection which deflates its seriousness and induces laughter.

Thus it happens that we should all feel scorn and indignation for Don Abbondio, for example, and hold Don Quijote to be a ridiculous fool and often a madman fit to be tied; nevertheless we are induced to pity, even to like, Don Abbondio, and to admire with infinite tenderness Don Quijote's ridiculous deeds, ennobled by such a high and pure ideal.

Where is the poet's feeling? In the scorn or in the pity for Don Abbondio? Manzoni has an abstract and very noble ideal of the priest's earthly mission, and he embodies this ideal in Federigo Borromeo. But reflection, a product of the humoristic temperament, suggests to the writer that this abstract ideal can be embodied only in rare exceptions and that human frailties are so plentiful. Had Manzoni listened only to the voice of the abstract ideal, he would have portrayed Don Abbondio in a way that we could only feel hate and scorn for him; but he listens within himself to the voice of human weaknesses. Because of his natural disposition, and because of his experience of life which has determined that disposition in him, Manzoni cannot help but split into two parts that ideal of religion and of the priesthood at the very moment of its conception; and, between the two brightly-lit flames of Fra Cristoforo and Cardinal Federigo, he sees, low on the ground, the shadow of Don Abbondio projecting itself, wary and sheepish. And at a certain moment Manzoni enjoys placing the active, affirmative feeling against the negating reflection, the flaming torch of feeling face to face with the icy water of reflection, in order to see how the exalted abstract sermons of altruism are doused by the rudimentary concrete arguments of the self.

Federigo Borromeo asks Don Abbondio:

And when you stood before the Church to accept this ministry, did she promise you safety for your life? Did she tell you that your pastoral duties would be free of all obstacles and exempt from all dangers? Did she perhaps tell you that duty would end where danger begins? Or didn't she tell you expressly the opposite? Did she not warn you that she was sending you forth like a lamb among the wolves? Did you not know that there were violent people who might be displeased by what you would be commanded to uphold? And He whose doctrine and example we follow, and in whose imitation we call ourselves and let ourselves be called shepherds, did He perhaps put as a condition the safety of His life when He descended upon earth to carry out His mission? And to save it, I mean, to preserve it a few days longer on earth, at the expense of charity and duty, was there a need for holy unction, for the imposition of hands, for priestly grace? Leave it to the world to advocate this virtue, to teach this doctrine. What am I saying? Oh, shame! The world itself rejects it: the world also makes its own laws, which prescribe evil as well as the good; the world has its own gospel, a gospel of pride and hatred; it will not have it said that the love of life is a reason for breaking the commandments. It does not want that and it is obeyed. And us—the children and messengers of the promise! What would the Church be if such language as yours were that of all your brethren? Where would she be if she had appeared in the world with such doctrines?[15]

Don Abbondio listens to this long and angry reprimand with his head bowed. Manzoni says that his soul "midst these arguments

15 *I promessi sposi*, Chap. XXV. [tr.]

was like a chick in the claws of a hawk, which hold it up in an unfamiliar region, in an air he had never before breathed." The simile is well put, although to some people the idea of the hawk's rapacity and fierceness has seemed somewhat unbecoming to Cardinal Federigo. The error, in my judgment, is not so much in the fact that the comparison may or may not be appropriate as in the comparison itself, which Manzoni likes and which, in his attempt to recreate Hesiod's little fable, has perhaps led him to say more than he should have. Was Don Abbondio really transported over an unfamiliar region during Cardinal Borromeo's arguments? But the comparison of the lamb among the wolves is found in the Gospel of Luke (X, 3), where Christ says these very words to his apostles: "Behold, I send you forth as lambs among the wolves." And who knows how many times Don Abbondio had read it; and, in other books, who knows how many times he had read those austere admonitions, and those edifying topics. We may also assume that Don Abbondio himself, when speaking or preaching abstractly on the priest's mission, would have said approximately the same things. And in fact, abstractly, he understands those things all too well: "My Most Illustrious Father, I suppose I am to blame," he in fact replies, though he hastens to add: "When one is expected not to take his life into account, I do not know what to say."

At that moment the Cardinal insists:

And don't you know that to suffer for the sake of justice is our victory? And if you don't know this, what do you preach? What are you a teacher of? What *glad tidings* do you bring to the poor? Who requires from you that you should overcome force with force? Surely you will not be asked one day if you were able to keep the powerful in check, for you were given neither mission nor means for that purpose. But you will assuredly be asked if you used the means you possessed to do what was required of you, even when they had the temerity to prohibit you from doing it.

"These saints also are very odd," Don Abbondio thinks. "The truth is, if we come right down to it, that they have more at heart the love between two young people than the life of a poor priest." And since the Cardinal has still the look of one who is expecting a reply, Don Abbondio says: "I repeat, Monsignor, I suppose I am in the wrong . . . But courage is not something one can give to oneself." Which really means: 'Yes, Most Eminent Grace, in theory you are right and I am to blame. But while your Eminence speaks so well, I am the one who saw those faces and heard those words.'

Finally, the Cardinal asks him: "Why, then, did you undertake a ministry which binds you to be constantly at strife with the passions of this world?"

The reason, alas, we know only too well: Manzoni himself told us at the very beginning of his novel; he insisted on telling us, although he could have just as well skipped it: Don Abbondio, neither noble nor rich, and even less courageous, realized, almost before reaching the age of reason, that he was, in that society, like a clay pot obliged to journey in the company of many iron pots. Hence he had quite willingly obeyed his parents, who wanted him to become a priest. The truth of the matter is that he had not thought much about the obligations and the noble aims of the ministry to which he was dedicating himself: to secure the means of living in relative comfort and to join a privileged and powerful class seemed to him two quite sufficient reasons for such a choice.

Don Abbondio at strife with the passions of his century? Why, he became a priest with the precise purpose of protecting himself from the onslaught of those very passions and of avoiding all conflicts with his own *particular system*.

It is necessary, dear readers, to listen also to the hare's reasons! Once I imagined that all the animals of the world would rush one by one to the den of the fox (or Sir Reynard, as he is known in the world of fable) as the news spread among them that the fox was planning to compose some counterfables in response to all the fables that men have been composing from time immemorial and in which the animals find good cause perhaps to feel slandered. And among the visitors to Sir Reynard's den came the hare to protest against the men who called him a coward, and he said: "I can tell you, Sir Reynard, that as far as I am concerned, I have always frightened away rats, lizards, birds, crickets, and many other small beasts: and if you were to ask them what they think of me, who knows what they would tell you, but they certainly would not say that I lack courage. Do humans expect that I should stand up on my hind legs in their presence and walk towards them so that they can capture and kill me? I sincerely believe, Sir Reynard, that the humans don't see any difference between heroism and stupidity."

Now, I do not deny that Don Abbondio is a hare. But we know that, whenever Don Rodrigo threatened, he did not threaten in vain; we know that he was truly capable of anything just "to get

to win the wager"; we know what those times were like, and we
can safely assume that, if Don Abbondio had married Renzo and
Lucia, certainly no one could have prevented him from being shot,
and that perhaps Lucia, a bride in name only, would have been
abducted upon leaving the church, and also that Renzo would have
been murdered. Of what avail were Fra Cristoforo's intervention
and advice? Isn't Lucia actually abducted from the Monza mon-
astery? There is, as Renzo says, a "league of scoundrels." To un-
ravel the entanglement, God's hand was needed; not just in a
manner of speaking, but truly God's hand. What could a poor
priest do?

Yes, Don Abbondio is indeed frightened; and De Sanctis has
left some marvelous pages on the sense of fear in the poor curate;
but he has undoubtedly overlooked one fact: that the fearful person is ridiculous and comical when he invents imaginary threats
and dangers; but when this person has a real *reason for being
afraid,* when we see a man caught and trapped in a terrifying conflict who by natural temperament and by education wants to
avoid all conflicts, even the minor ones, and who should be in-
volved out of sacred duty in that terrifying conflict, this fearful
person is no longer merely comical. For that situation, not even a
hero like Fra Cristoforo, who goes to face his enemy in his own
little palace, is sufficient. Don Abbondio does not have the courage
of his own duty; but this duty is made difficult by other people's
evil deeds; consequently, that courage is anything but easy, and to
achieve it a hero would be needed. In the place of a hero we find
Don Abbondio. We can become indignant with him only abstractly,
only, that is, if we consider his priestly ministry in the abstract. Of
course we would have admired a priest-hero who, in Don Abbondio's place, would have disregarded the threat and danger and
would have fulfilled the obligations of his ministry. And yet we
cannot help but feel pity for Don Abbondio, who is not the hero
that would have been needed in his situation and who not only
lacks the extraordinary courage that was required, but has no
courage at all; and *courage is not something one can give to oneself!*

A superficial observer will notice the laughter which rises from
the external comical quality of Don Abbondio's actions, gestures,
reticent phrases, etc., and will immediately classify him as a
ridiculous or simply a comical figure. But the reader who is not
satisfied with this superficiality and is capable of penetrating to a

deeper level, will feel that the laughter stems from quite a different source and is not simply the laughter of comic situations.

Don Abbondio is one who is in a situation in place of the person the situation calls for. Manzoni, however, is not irritated by the reality he finds, because, although he has, as we said, a lofty ideal of the priesthood, he has also reflection which advises him that this ideal is embodied only in very rare exceptions, and thus reflection constrains him to limit that ideal, as De Sanctis observes. Now, what is this limitation of the ideal? It is precisely the effect of reflection which, by exerting itself upon the ideal, has suggested the feeling of the opposite to the artist. And precisely this feeling of the opposite is objectified and living in Don Abbondio. Therefore, he is not simply comical, but genuinely and profoundly humoristic.

Kindliness? Sympathetic indulgence? A word of caution: let us abandon these notions, which are essentially alien and superficial, and which, should we review them in depth, may well lead us, here again, to the discovery of the opposite. Shall we try to see how? Yes, Manzoni sympathizes with that poor fellow Don Abbondio; but it is a sympathy, dear readers, that, by necessity, tortures him at the same time. In fact, only by laughing at him and by making the readers laugh at him, can he sympathize with him and make him a sympathetic character, feel pity for him and make the reader feel pity for him. But by simultaneously laughing at him and feeling sympathy for him, Manzoni is also laughing bitterly at our helpless human nature that is afflicted with so many frailties; the more the considerations of pity are linked together to protect the poor curate, the more the discrediting of human value extends all around him. The poet, in short, induces us to feel sympathy for the poor curate by having us recognize that, if we look deep within our conscience, all that Don Abbondio feels and experiences is after all human, common to all of us. And what follows from that? What follows is that—if, by virtue of itself, this particular feeling becomes general, if this mixed emotion of laughter and sorrow, the more it narrows and defines itself in Don Abbondio, the more it extends and almost evaporates into an infinite sadness—what follows, we were saying, is that if we consider the figure of Manzoni's priest from this point of view, we are no longer able to laugh at him. That pity, in the end, is pitiless: the sympathetic indulgence is not as good-natured as it seems at first glance.

It is an extraordinary thing, as we can see, to have an ideal—a religious one, in Manzoni's case, a chivalric one, in Cervantes' case—only then to see it reduced by reflection in Don Abbondio and in Don Quijote! Manzoni finds comfort from that by creating, beside the village priest, Fra Cristoforo and Cardinal Borromeo; but it is also true that, since he is above all a humorist, his most vivid creature is the other one, that is, the one in which the feeling of the opposite has been embodied. Cervantes cannot in any way find comfort because, in the Manchegan jailhouse, as he himself says, he creates in Don Quijote *someone who resembles him.*

V

It is a superficial and one-sided view, we said, to see in humor a particular contrast between ideals and reality. There may well be, we repeat, an ideal: this depends on the poet's temperament; but if there is one, it exists only to see itself taken apart, limited, and represented in this manner. To be sure, like all the other elements that make up the spirit of a poet, the ideal enters and makes itself felt in the work of humor, and gives it a particular character, a particular flavor; but it is not an indispensable condition: on the contrary, it is the humorist's nature, due to the special activity that reflection acquires in him by giving rise to the feeling of the opposite, to be in a state of mind of no longer knowing where to turn, of perplexity and irresoluteness.

This is precisely what distinguishes the humorist sharply from the comic writer, the ironist, and the satirist. The feeling of the opposite does not arise in any of the latter; if it did, the laughter provoked in the comic writer by the perception of any abnormality would turn bitter and therefore would no longer be comical; the contradiction which in irony is only verbal, between what the writer says and what he wants understood, would become real and substantial, and therefore would no longer be ironic; and the scorn, or at least the aversion, for reality, which is the reason of any satire, would cease to exist. Not that, however, the humorist likes reality! The slightest liking for it would be enough for reflection to exert itself upon it and to ruin it for him.

Sharp and subtle, reflection insinuates itself everywhere and disassembles everything: every image born of feeling, every ideal fiction, every appearance of reality, every illusion. Human thought, Guy de Maupassant used to say, "turns around and around like

a fly in a bottle." All phenomena either are illusory or their reason is inexplicable and escapes us. Our knowledge of the world
and of ourselves totally lacks the objective value which we usually
presume to attribute to it. This objective value of reality is a
continuous illusory fabrication. Shall we then witness the struggle
between illusion, which also insinuates itself everywhere and builds
things up in its own way, and humoristic reflection, which disassembles those constructions one by one?

Let us begin with the construction that illusion builds for each
of us, that is, the construction that each of us makes of himself
through the work of illusion. Do we see ourselves in our true and
genuine reality, as we really are, or rather as what we should like
to be? By means of a spontaneous internal device, a product of
secret tendencies and unconscious imitation, do we not in good
faith believe ourselves to be different from what we essentially
are? And we think, act, and live according to this fictitious, and
yet sincere, interpretation of ourselves.

Now reflection, indeed, can reveal this illusory construction to
the comic writer and to the satirist as well as to the humorist. But
the comic writer will merely laugh, being content to deflate this
metaphor of ourselves created by spontaneous illusion; the satirist
will feel disdain towards it; the humorist does neither: through
the ridiculousness of the discovery, he will see the serious and painful side; he will disassemble the construction, but not solely to
laugh at it; and, instead of feeling disdain, he will rather, in his
laughter, feel compassion.

The comic writer and the satirist know through reflection how
much dribble the spider of experience draws from social life in
weaving the web of mentality in this or that individual, and they
know how the so-called moral sense often gets entangled in this
web. What are, after all, the social relationships of our so-
called convenience? Considerations based on calculation, in which
morality is almost always sacrificed. The humorist delves more
deeply, and he laughs without becoming irritated when he discovers how men ingenuously and in all good faith, through the
working of a spontaneous fiction, are induced to interpret as authentic feeling and as true moral sense what is really nothing more
than a consideration or a moral sense based on convenience, that
is, on calculation. And delving still more deeply, he discovers that
even the need that men have to appear worse than they really are
can become conventional, if having joined some social group re-

quires that they display the ideals and feelings which are peculiarly natural to that group but which, to those who participate, will seem contrary and inferior to their own inner feelings.[16]

The conciliation of jarring tendencies, of conflicting feelings, of contrary opinions seems more effectively achieved by means of a common lie than by the explicit and openly stated tolerance of dissent and conflict. In other words, it seems that lying is to be considered more advantageous than telling the truth, insofar as the former can unite where the latter divides; and this does not prevent men, while tacitly uncovering and recognizing falsehood, from using veracity as a guarantee of the associative effectiveness of falsehood, by making hypocrisy look like sincerity.

Reserve, secrecy, the practice of letting others believe more than one says or does, even silence when not separated from the knowledge of the signs that can justify it (as in the unforgettable Count Zio of the Secret Council),[17] are all artifices frequently used in everyday life. And so is the artifice of not allowing others to understand what we are thinking, of letting others believe that we are thinking less than we actually are, and of claiming that others see us as different from what we really are. Rousseau, in *Emile*, observed:

As soon as we find ourselves capable of doing what we should not do, we try to hide our misdeeds. When one interest makes us promise something, a greater interest can make us violate the promise: what really matters is that the violation be carried out with impunity. The resource is natural: we conceal our thoughts and actions and we lie . . . There are two kinds of falsehoods: one relating to matters of fact which have to do with the past, and one relating to matters of right and regarding the future. The first takes place when we deny having done what we actually have done or when we claim that we have done what we have not done, and generally when we speak knowingly against the truth of fact. The second takes place when we promise what we have no intention

16 Here I base myself on the perceptive notions of Giovanni Marchesini, *Le finzioni dell'anima* (Bari: Laterza, 1905).

17 *I promessi sposi*, Chap. XVIII: "An ambiguous way of speaking, a skillful use of silence and of leaving things half unsaid, a straining of the eyes that suggested an inability to speak, a manner of enticing without promising anything and of using polite words to cloak a threat—these were all directed to that end and they were all, to one degree or another, used to his advantage, even to the point that a statement like 'I can do nothing in this case,' which was spoken in truth but said unconvincingly, served to increase his reputation, and therefore the effectiveness of his power, like those boxes still to be seen in some pharmacies that carry inscriptions in Arabic on the outside and have nothing inside, but which serve to keep up the credibility of those shops."

of keeping and in general when we declare our intentions to be opposite to what they actually are.[18]

It is clear that, in both cases, falsehood arises from the interests and the relations of convenience, as a means of keeping the favor and good will of others and of securing their help.[19] The more difficult the struggle for life is and the more one's own weakness is felt in this struggle, the greater the need becomes for mutual deceit. The simulation of strength, of honesty, of sympathy, of prudence—in short, of all the highest qualities of truthfulness—is a form of adaptation, a skillful weapon. The humorist readily perceives the various simulations used in the struggle for life; he amuses himself by unmasking them, but he does not become indignant: it's the truth!

While the sociologist describes social life as it appears from external manifestations, the humorist, armed with his keen intuition, reveals how profoundly different the outer appearances are from what takes place in the inner consciousness. Yet we lie psychologically just as we lie socially. And, since conscious life extends only to the surface of our psychic being, lying to ourselves is a result of social lying. The soul that reflects upon itself is a solitary soul, but this inner solitude is never so great that the suggestions from collective life, with its typical dissimulations and transfigurative devices, do not penetrate the consciousness.

There lives in our soul the soul of the race or of the community of which we are a part. We unconsciously feel the pressure of other people's way of judging, feeling, and acting; and as simulation and dissimulation dominate in the social world—the more habitual they become, the less they are noticed—we too simulate and dissimulate with ourselves, doubling and often even multiplying ourselves. We, as individuals, experience something which is inherent and essential to social living, the vanity of seeming different from what we really are, and we avoid any analysis which, unveiling our vanity, would prompt our remorse and humiliate us before ourselves. But it is the humorist who does this analysis for us and who can also take up the task of unmasking all vanities and of depicting society, as Thackeray himself did, as a *Vanity Fair*.[20]

---

[18] Jean Jacques Rousseau, *Emile*, Bk. II. [tr.]

[19] In the original text, this sentence is erroneously included in the quotation from Rousseau. [tr.]

[20] Thackeray takes up the same task in his *Book of Snobs* and in his *Vanity Fair: A Novel Without a Hero*, full of scenes of all sorts, "brilliantly illuminated with the Author's own candles," as he himself says in the introduction.

Moreover, the humorist is well aware that the claim that man has a logical mind is much too exaggerated if compared with his actual logical coherence, and that, if we imagine ourselves as capable of logical thought on the speculative level, the logic of our action can belie the logic of our thought and show that it is fictitious to believe in its absolute sincerity. Habit, unconscious imitation, mental laziness, all contribute in creating the misunderstanding. And even if we should hold closely to a rigorously logical reason with, let's say, the respect and love for certain ideals, is the connection that we make between these ideals and reason always sincere? Is pure and disinterested reason always the true and exclusive source of the selection of ideals and of our perseverence in cultivating them? Or is it not more consistent with reality to suspect that sometimes they are evaluated not by an objective and rational criterion, but by special emotional impulses and obscure tendencies?

The barriers, the limits that we set on our consciousness are also illusions; they are the conditions through which our relative individuality manifests itself, but actually they do not exist at all. We live in ourselves not only as we are now, but also as we were in the past; and as such, we live and feel and reason with thoughts and emotions which are, in our present consciousness, obscured and obliterated by the long period of forgetfulness, but which, as a result of a shock or a sudden turmoil of the spirit, can still give sign of life and reveal another unsuspected being within our present self. The limits of our personal and conscious memory are not absolute limits. Beyond that line there are further memories, perceptions, and reasonings. What we know of ourselves is only a fraction, perhaps a very small fraction, of what we are.[21] At certain exceptional moments we come upon so many surprising things within ourselves—perceptions, reasonings, states of consciousness —which really lie beyond the relative limits of our normal and conscious existence. Certain ideals, which we think are no longer in us and no longer capable of exerting any influence on our thoughts, emotions and actions, perhaps are still alive in us, if not in their pure, intellectual form, at least in their substratum which consists of emotional and practical tendencies. And it may

[21] See that survey of remarkable psycho-physiological experiments in Alfred Binet's book, *Les altérations de la personnalité* (Paris: Alcan, 1892), from which these statements and many others can be cited, as Gaetano Negri has observed in "Il problema dello spiritismo," in his *Segni dei tempi*, 3rd ed. (Milan: Hoepli, 1903), pp. 325–369.

be that certain tendencies from which we believe to have freed ourselves are still real motives for action, while certain new beliefs which we hold to be truly and intimately ours have no practical influence on us other than illusory.

And precisely the various tendencies that mark the personality lead us seriously to think that the individual soul is not *one*. How can we claim that it is *one*, in fact, if passion and reason, instinct and will, tendencies and ideals constitute as many separate and mobile systems functioning in such a way that the individual— living now one of them, now another, and now some compromise between two or more psychic tendencies—appears as if he really has within himself several different and even opposed souls, several different and conflicting personalities? Pascal observed that there is no man who differs from another man more than he differs, with the passing of time, from himself.[22]

The oneness of the soul contradicts the historical concept of the human soul. Its life is a changing equilibrium; it is a continual awakening and obliterating of emotions, tendencies, and ideas; an incessant fluctuating between contradictory terms, and an oscillating between such extremes as hope and fear, truth and falsehood, beauty and ugliness, right and wrong, etc. If in the obscure view of the future a bright plan of action suddenly appears or the flower of pleasure is vaguely seen to shine, soon there also appears our memory of the past, often dim and sad, to avenge the rights of experience; or our sulky and unruly sense of the present will intervene to restrain our spirited imagination. This conflict of memories, hopes, forebodings, perceptions, and ideals, can be seen as a struggle of various souls which are all fighting among themselves for the exclusive and final power over our personality.

Here is a high ranking functionary who believes himself to be— and who, poor fellow, actually is—a man of honor. In him the moral soul dominates; yet one fine day the instinctive soul, which is like a primal beast crouched deep inside us, kicks out the moral soul and this honest man steals. Now the poor fellow himself, shortly afterwards, will be stunned at his own action, and will weep and ask himself in despair: 'How could I have every done such a thing?' But, yes indeed, he has stolen. And what about that other man? He is an honorable man, indeed most honorable: well, he has

---

[22] Cf. Blaise Pascal's thoughts on the self in *Oeuvres Complètes*, ed. L. Lafuma (Paris, 1963), particularly Nos. 597, 668, 673, 688, 806, 978, and the famous texts on imagination (No. 44) and diversion (No. 136). [tr.]

committed murder. The moral ideal constituted in him a soul which was in contrast with the instinctive soul and to some extent also with the emotional or passional soul; it formed an acquired soul which fought the hereditary soul, which, left free to itself for a short while, suddenly committed robbery and murder.

Life is a continual flux which we try to stop, to fix in stable and determined forms, both inside and outside ourselves, because we are already fixed forms, forms which move in the midst of other immobile forms and which however can follow the flow of life until the movement, gradually slowing and becoming more and more rigid, eventually ceases. The forms in which we seek to stop, to fix in ourselves this constant flux are the concepts, the ideals with which we would like consistently to comply, all the fictions we create for ourselves, the conditions, the state in which we tend to stabilize ourselves. But within ourselves, in what we call the soul and is the life in us, the flux continues, indistinct under the barriers and beyond the limits we impose as a means to fashion a consciousness and a personality for ourselves. In certain moments of turmoil all these fictitious forms are hit by the flux and collapse miserably under its thrust; and even what does not flow under the barriers and beyond the limits—that which is distinctly clear to us and which we have carefully channelled into our feelings, into the duties we have imposed upon ourselves, into the habits we have marked out for ourselves—in certain moments of floodtide, overflows and upsets everything.

There are restless souls, almost in a continuous state of fusion, who are disdainful of becoming congealed or solidified into a particular form of personality. But even for the more peaceful souls, who have settled into one form or other, fusion is always possible: the flux of life is in all of us.

This is why, moreover, our bodies, forever fixed as they are in immutable features while our souls flow and change into new forms, can sometimes be a torture for all of us. While looking at ourselves in the mirror, we sometimes ask ourselves: 'Exactly why are we made just like this, with this particular face and this particular body?' We lift a hand unconsciously, and that gesture remains suspended. It seems strange that *we* did it. *We see ourselves live.* In that suspended gesture we can liken ourselves to a statue; to that statue of an ancient orator, for instance, whom we see in a niche as we go up the stairs of the Quirinale. He has a scroll in one hand and is holding out the other hand in a moderate gesture:

how grieved and surprised he seems for having been there through the centuries, fixed in stone, suspended in that posture and facing so many people that have climbed, are climbing, and will climb those stairs!

In certain moments of inner silence, in which our soul strips itself of all its habitual fictions and our eyes become sharper and more piercing, we see ourselves in life, and life in itself, as if in a barren and disquieting nakedness; we are seized by a strange impression, as if, in a flash, we could clearly perceive a reality different from the one that we normally perceive, a reality living beyond the reach of human vision, outside the forms of human reason. Very lucidly, then, the texture of daily existence, almost suspended in the void of our inner silence, seems meaningless, devoid of purpose; and that new reality appears to us dreadful in its sternly detached and mysterious crudeness, for all our usual fictitious relationships, both of feelings and images, have separated and disintegrated in it. The inner void expands, surpasses the limits of our body, and becomes a weird emptiness that engulfs us as if time and life had come to a stop, as if our inner silence had plunged into the abyss of mystery. With a supreme effort we then try to recapture the normal consciousness of things, to renew our usual relationships with them, to reassemble our ideas and to feel alive again in the usual way. But we can no longer trust this normal consciousness, these newly recollected ideas and this habitual sense of living because we now know that they are deceptions which we use in order to survive and that underneath them there is something else which man can face only at the cost of either death or insanity. It was only an instant; but its impression lasts for a long time, as a sort of dizziness which contrasts with the stability, itself so illusory, of things: ambitious or miserable appearances. And life, the small usual life that roams among these appearances, almost seems to us no longer to be real; it is like a mechanical phantasmagoria. How could we give importance to it? How could we respect it?

Today we exist, tomorrow we will not. What face have we been given in order to play the part of the living? An ugly nose? How wearisome to have to walk around with an ugly nose the rest of our life. . . . Lucky that, in the long run, we no longer notice it. But other people do notice it, even when we have come to believe that we have a handsome nose; and when this happens, we can no longer understand why they laugh when they look at us. They

are such fools! Let's console ourselves by looking at someone else's
ears and someone else's lips. They don't even realize what kind of
ears and lips they have and yet they have the nerve to laugh at us.
Masks, they are all masks—a puff and they are gone, to make room
for other masks. Take that poor cripple over there, for instance
. . . who is he? A rush towards death on crutches . . . In one case,
life may crush someone's foot; in another case, it may pluck out
someone's eye; a wooden leg, a glass eye, and onward! Everybody
straightens up his mask the best he can—that is, the external mask,
for we also have the inner mask, which often is at variance with
the outer one. And nothing is true! Oh yes, the sea is true, the
mountain is true; the stone, the blade of grass are true; but man?
Unwillingly, unknowingly, he is always wearing the mask of whatever it is that he, in good faith, fancies himself to be: *handsome,
good, courteous, generous, unhappy,* etc. etc. To think of it, all
this is so ludicrous. Yes, because a dog, let's say—what does
a dog do when the first fever of life has left him? He eats and
sleeps; he lives as he can and as he must live: he closes his eyes,
patiently, and lets time go by and takes the weather as it comes,
cold if it is cold, hot if it is hot; and if they kick him, he takes it
because this, too, is something that falls to his lot. But man? Even
when he is old, he always has that *fever;* he is delirious and does
not realize it; he cannot help assuming a pose, somehow, even in
front of himself, and with his imagination he creates so many
things which he needs to believe in and to take seriously.

He is helped in this by a certain devilish little machine that
nature chose to give him and to fix inside him as a signal proof of
her benevolence. For the sake of their well-being, men should have
left it to rust without ever moving or touching it. But, instead,
certain men showed such pride and deemed themselves so lucky
to have it that they immediately set out, with dogged zeal, to make
it perfect. Aristotle even wrote a book about it, a graceful little
treatise, which is still used in the schools, so that the youngsters
may learn early and well how to play with it. It is a kind of filter
pump that connects the brain to the heart. LOGIC is what our
revered philosophers call it.

The brain uses it to pump the emotions from the heart and to
extract ideas from them. In passing through its filter, the emotions
leave behind whatever they contain that is heated and troubled:
they cool, purify, and i•de•al•ize themselves. Thus, a poor emotion—which initially is evoked by a particular event or by circum-

stances that are often painful—becomes a generalized and abstract idea once it is pumped and filtered by the brain through the little machine. What happens then? What happens is that not only do we have to suffer the grief of a particular event or a temporary misfortune, but we must also poison our lives with the concentrated extract and corrosive sublimate of logical deduction. And there are many wretched people who think that in this way they can cure themselves of all the ills of the world, and so they continually pump and filter until their hearts become as dry as cork and their brain is like a druggist's shelf full of little bottles which carry, on black labels, the word POISON over skull and crossbones.

Man does not have an absolute idea or conception of life, but rather a feeling that changes and varies depending on the times, the circumstances, and luck. Now logic, by abstracting ideas from emotions, tends precisely to fix what is changeable and fluid. It tends to give an absolute value to what is relative, and thus it aggravates an ill which is already serious in itself since the prime root of our ills consists precisely in this feeling that we have of life. The tree lives and does not feel itself alive: from its standpoint, the earth, the sun, the air, the light, the wind, and the rain, are not things it differs from. Man, instead, is given at birth the sad privilege of feeling himself alive, with the fine illusion that results from it: that of taking this inner feeling, changeable and varying, as something that really exists outside of himself.

The ancients created the myth in which Prometheus stole a spark from the sun to give it as a gift to men. Now our feeling of life is precisely this Promethean spark of the fable. It causes us to see ourselves as lost on earth; it projects all around us a more or less wide ring of light, beyond which is all a dark shadow, a frightening shadow that would not exist if we did not have that spark lit within us, a shadow, nonetheless, that we must, unfortunately, believe to be real, as long as the spark keeps alive in our breasts. And, when it is at last extinguished by the blow of death, will we really be received by that fictitious shadow, will we be received by the eternal night following the misty day of our illusion, or is it not more likely that we will be left to the mercy of Being, which will have shattered only the vain forms of human reason? All that shadow, that enormous mystery, which so many philosophers have vainly speculated about and which now science, even though it refuses to investigate it, does not exclude—could it perhaps not be, after all, a deception like any other, a deception of our minds, a fantasy which does not acquire any coloration? What if all this mystery, in short, did not exist outside of us, but only in us, and unavoidably so on account of our famous privilege, the feeling that we have of life? What if death were only the breath that extinguishes this feeling in us, a feeling so painful and terrifying because it is limited and defined by that ring of fictitious shadow beyond the slight circle of faint light which we project around us and in which our life remains as if imprisoned, as if excluded for some time from eternal and universal life, which it seems to us that we shall one day rejoin, whereas we are already in it and shall forever remain in it, but without this sense of exile that grieves us? Here again, is it not possible that the limits of our individuality are illusory and have to do with our dim-sightedness? Perhaps we have always lived and shall always live with the universe; perhaps even now, in our present form, we participate in all the manifestations of the universe: we do not know it, we do not see it because unfortunately the spark that Prometheus chose to give us enables us to see only within the small sphere of light that it casts.

Tomorrow a humorist could picture Prometheus on the Caucasus in the act of pondering sadly his lit torch and perceiving in it, at last, the fateful cause of his infinite torment. He has finally realized that Jupiter is no more than a vain phantasm, a pitiable deception, the shadow of his own body projecting itself as a giant in the sky, precisely because of the lighted torch he holds in his hand. Jupiter could disappear only on one condition, on condition that Prometheus extinguish his candle, that is, his torch. But he does not know how, he does not want to, he cannot; and so the shadow remains, terrifying and tyrannical, for all men who fail to realize the fateful deception.

Thus the contrast reveals itself to be irreparable and its conflicting elements prove as inseparable as the shadow from the body. In this rapid vision of humor we have seen it expand gradually, go beyond the limits of our individual being, where it is rooted, and extend itself all around us. It was discovered by reflection, which sees in everything an illusory or feigned or fictitious construction of our emotions and disassembles and unmakes it with a keen, subtle and detailed analysis.

One of the greatest humorists, though himself unaware of it, was Copernicus who, properly speaking, disassembled not the machine of the universe but the haughty image we had formed of it for ourselves. Read that dialogue of Leopardi's which bears as a title precisely the name of the Polish canon.

It was the discovery of the telescope which dealt us the *coup de grâce:* another infernal little mechanism which could pair up with the one nature chose to bestow upon us. But we invented this one so as not to be inferior. While our eye looks from below through the smaller lens, and sees as big all that nature had providentially wanted for us to see small, what does our soul do? It jumps up to look from above through the larger lens, and as a consequence the telescope becomes a terrible instrument, which sinks the earth and man and all our glories and greatness.

Fortunately, it is in the nature of humoristic reflection to provoke the feeling of the opposite, which in this case says: 'But is man really as small as he looks when we see him through an inverted telescope? If he can understand and conceive of his infinite smallness, it means that he understands and conceives of the infinite greatness of the universe. How, then, can one say that man is small?'

But it is also true that, if he feels big and a humorist finds out, he may end up like Gulliver, a giant in Lilliput and a toy in the hands of the giants of Brobdingnag.

VI

From what we have said up to now about the special activity of reflection in the humorist, we can clearly see what the intimate process of the art of humor must necessarily be.

Art, like all ideal or illusory constructions, also tends to fix life; it fixes it in one moment or in various given moments—the statue in a gesture, the landscape in a temporary immutable perspective. But—what about the perpetual mobility of successive perspectives? What about the constant flow in which souls are?

Art generally abstracts and concentrates; that is, it catches and represents the essential and characteristic ideality of both men and things. Now it seems to the humorist that all this oversimplifies nature and tends to make life too reasonable or at least too coherent. It seems to him that art does not take into account, as it should, the causes, the *real* causes that often move this poor human soul to the most mindless and totally unpredictable actions. For the humorist, the causes in real life are never as logical and as well ordered as they are in our common works of art, in which, basically, everything is arranged, organized and ordered according to the writer's proposed objective. Order? Coherence? But if we have within ourselves four or five different souls—the instinctive, the moral, the emotional, the social—constantly fighting among themselves? The attitude of our consciousness is contingent upon whichever of these souls is dominant; and we hold as valid and sincere that fictitious interpretation of ourselves, of our inner being—a being that we know nothing about because it never reveals itself in its entirety but now in one way and now in another way, according to the turn of the circumstances of life.

Yes, an epic or dramatic poet may represent a hero of his in whom opposite and contrasting elements are shown in conflict, but he will *compose* a character from these elements and will want to represent him as consistent in every action. Well, the humorist does just the opposite: he will *decompose* the character into his elements and while the epic or dramatic poet takes pains to picture him as coherent in every action, the humorist enjoys representing him in his incongruities.

The humorist does not recognize heroes, or rather he lets others represent them. For his part, he knows what a legend is and how it is created, what history is and how it is made: they are all compositions, more or less ideal; and the greater the pretense of reality, the more idealized they are. The humorist amuses himself by disassembling these compositions, although one cannot say that it is a pleasant amusement.

The humorist sees the world, not exactly in the nude but, so to speak, in shirt sleeves. He sees a king in his shirt sleeves, a king who makes such a fine impression when we see him composed in the majesty of his throne, with his crown, sceptre, and mantle of purple and ermine. And please don't compose the dead with too much pomp on their catafalques in the funeral chambers, because he is capable of not respecting even this composition, all this organized display. For example, in the corpse, which lies there cold and stiff but dressed up with decorations and tail-coat, the humorist is capable of unexpectedly overhearing, while everyone is standing there in grief, some mournful belly-grumble, and of exclaiming in Latin (for certain things are best expressed in Latin): *Digestio post mortem.*

Also those Austrian soldiers in Giusti's poem, which we discussed at the beginning, are in the end seen by the poet as so many poor men in shirtsleeves: the poet, that is, comes to consider them without their hateful uniforms, in which he sees the symbol of his enslaved homeland. In the poet's mind, those uniforms make up an ideal representation of his enslaved homeland until humoristic reflection unmakes this representation, unclothes the soldiers and sees in them a crowd of poor men, grieved and mocked. In his *Sartor Resartus,* Carlyle says that "man is a dressed animal" and that "society is founded upon cloth."[23] And cloth is also something that *composes* and *conceals,* two things which humor cannot stand.

Bare life, nature without any order, at least without any apparent order, bristling with contradictions, seems to the humorist to be very far from the ideal contrivances of ordinary artistic creations, in which all the elements are visibly held together in close interaction and collaboration.

In real life the actions which make a character stand out are set against a background of ordinary events and common details. Well, writers in general do not avail themselves of these events and details, or they do not pay much attention to them, as if they had no value or were useless and insignificant. The humorist instead treasures them. Isn't gold found, in nature, mixed with earth? Well, writers usually discard the earth and present the gold in the form of new coins, duly smelted and cast, duly weighed and stamped with their brand and hallmark. But the humorist knows that the ordinary happenings, the commonplace details—in short, the material substance of life, so varied and complex—harshly contradict those ideal simplifications; he knows that they incite actions and inspire thoughts and feelings that are contrary to all that harmonious logic of acts and characters created by the ordinary writers. And what about the unpredictable element in life? What about the abyss which exists in our souls? Don't we often feel within ourselves the flashes of strange thoughts, like flashes of madness, inconsequential thoughts we dare not confide even to ourselves, as if really issuing from a soul different from the one we normally recognize as ours? Hence comes, in the art of humor, all that searching of the most intimate and minute details—which may appear trivial or vulgar if compared with the idealized syntheses of art in general—and that search of contrasts and contradictions which is at the basis of the art of the humorist as opposed to the consistency sought by others; hence all that is disorganized, unraveled and whimsical, all the digressions which can

---

[23] Cf. Thomas Carlyle, *Sartor Resartus,* I, Chaps. I, VIII. [tr.]

be seen in the works of humor, as opposed to the ordered construction, the *composition* of the works of art in general.

These traits are the result of reflection which dissects. 'If Cleopatra's nose had been longer, who knows what other events the world might have experienced.' This *if*—this minute particle which can be pinned to, and inserted like a wedge into, all events —can produce many different disruptions and disarrangements; it can cause many decompositions when used by a humorist who, like Sterne, for example, sees the whole world regulated by that which is infinitely small.

To sum up: humor consists in the feeling of the opposite produced by the special activity of reflection, which does not remain hidden and does not become, as usual in art, a form of feeling, but its opposite, though it follows closely behind the feeling as the shadow follows the body. The ordinary artist pays attention only to the body; the humorist pays attention to both, and sometimes more to the shadow than to the body: he notices all the tricks of the shadow, the way it sometimes grows longer and sometimes short and squat, almost as if to mimic the body, which meanwhile is indifferent to it and does not pay any attention to it.

In the medieval comic representations of the devil we find a student who mocks him by having him catch his own shadow on the wall. Whoever made this representation of the devil was certainly no humorist. The humorist well knows how valuable a shadow may be: take *Peter Schlemihl's* word for it.

INDEX

147